Essentials

ABSOLUTE

FOR GUITAR

of

Music

Theory

Text editing by: Jeneane McKenzie

Library and Archives Canada Cataloguing in Publication

MacLean, Don J., 1968-
        Absolute essentials of music theory for guitar / Don J. MacLean ; editor, Jeneane McKenzie.

Includes index.
ISBN 1-896595-32-4

        1. Music theory--Elementary works. I. McKenzie, Jeneane, 1968- II. Title.

MT7.M1592 2004   781   C2004-
904734-5

Quantity discounts are available on bulk purchases of this book for educational purposes. For information please contact Agogic Publishing 406-109 Tenth Street, New Westminster, British Columbia, V3M 3X7, tel. (604) 290-2692, fax (604) 540-4419.

Visit us on our website:
http://www.agogic.biz
for free downloads
and product information.

Contents

Chapter 5   Harmonized Scales

Chapter 6   Rhythm

Conclusion

Index

About the Author

Don J. MacLean is an active freelance guitarist, composer and educator. His musical training includes studies at the Royal Conservatory of Music, Humber College, and York University, where he obtained his B.A. (Dbl. Hons. Maj.) in music and psychology. His twenty years of teaching, performing and composing have made Don a highly sought-after expert for workshops, seminars and master classes.

Don J. MacLean is the author of:

The World of Scales: A Compendium of Scales for the Modern Guitar Player
The World of Scales: A Compendium of Scales for all Instruments

Guitar Essentials: Chord Master
Guitar Essentials: Chord Master Expanded Edition
Guitar Essentials: Scale Master 1
Guitar Essentials: Scale Master Expanded Edition
Guitar Essentials: Improviser
Guitar Essentials: Music Theory

Music Essentials: Improviser

Absolute Essentials of Music Theory
Absolute Essentials of Music Theory for Guitar
Absolute Essentials of Guitar

Guitar Quick Start

Fit Fingers Book 1
Fit Fingers Book 2

Quick Tips for Faster Fingers
Quick Tips: Guitar Chords 101
Quick Tips: Guitar Technique 101

Mega Chops: Scale Mastery Beyond Hanon
Mega Chops: Guitar Technique Volume 1
Mega Chops: Guitar Technique Volume 2
Mega Chops: Guitar Technique Volume 3

Introduction

Music theory codifies the techniques that have been used by composers for hundreds of years. Why reinvent the wheel when you can learn from the masters? Music theory will provide you with many tools that will not only increase your understanding of music, but will also give you extensive resources for writing your own songs.

There are currently many, many, music theory books available, but very few are easily accessible for the contemporary guitarist. This book has been written to address this issue. Theoretical concepts are only as good as their application. As you learn new theoretical concepts you need to be able to see how they can be applied to the guitar. In each chapter of this book you will find application sections that describe how to apply each theoretical concept to the fretboard of the guitar.

The **Absolute Essentials of Music Theory for Guitar**, has been written to provide the beginner to intermediate guitar player, of all styles, with the absolute essentials of music theory. Each chapter begins with an explanation of theoretical concepts and concludes with questions and answers that will test your new knowledge.

How to Use This Book

It is best to work your way through each chapter of this book in sequential order. Each chapter builds upon the information presented in earlier chapters. Chapter 6 "Rhythm" is the exception and can be consulted at any time.

As you progress through the Absolute Essentials of Music Theory for Guitar, be sure to spend some time reviewing earlier chapters. Feel free to come up with your own questions to test your knowledge. Also, be on the lookout for opportunities to apply your knowledge—this is one of the keys to retaining information. The wider the application of the concepts presented in this book, the greater your retention and understanding will be. Be sure to apply each concept to the guitar.

Chapter 1

Basics

Properties of Sound

Musical notes, although they may be produced by different instruments, all produce the same result—a series of alternating increases and decreases in air pressure. These vibrations are picked up by our ear drums (tympanic membranes) and are transmitted to areas of the brain where we process sound. The result is the music we hear. **Pitch** refers to the relative highness or lowness of a note. **Frequency**, the number of vibrations per second, is measured in units called **Hertz** (Hz). One Hertz is equal to one vibration per second. As frequency increases so does pitch—the highest note on an acoustic piano is 4186 Hz and the lowest is 27.5 Hz.

Music Notation

Music notation is used to indicate both the pitch and duration of a note. Notes are written on a set of parallel lines called a **staff**. The vertical position of a note on the staff indicates its pitch.

⇑
Higher

Lower
⇓

Bar Line

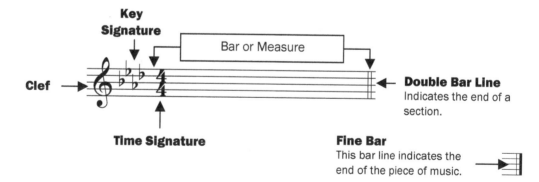

Key Signature

Bar or Measure

Clef →

Double Bar Line
Indicates the end of a section.

Time Signature

Fine Bar
This bar line indicates the end of the piece of music.

The first symbol you encounter in printed music is called a clef. A **clef** is a symbol used to indicate the pitch of a particular line. Once you know the pitch of one note you can easily derive the others. The musical alphabet consists of the first seven letters of the alphabet: A—B—C—D—E—F—G.

The two most common clefs are the treble and bass clefs. Guitar music is notated in the treble clef and will therefore be our main focus. The **treble clef**, is sometimes called the "G" clef because it indicates the position of the note G. An easy way to remember the notes in the treble clef is to use the following mnemonics:

Every **G**ood **B**oy **D**eserves **F**udge (notes on lines)

FACE (notes in spaces)

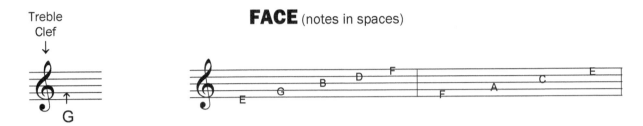

The **bass clef** is also called the "F" clef because it indicates the position of the note F. An easy way to remember the notes in the bass clef is to use the following mnemonics:

Good **B**oys **D**eserve **F**udge **A**lways (notes on lines)

All **C**ows **E**at **G**rass (notes in spaces)

To write notes that are found below or above the staff, ledger lines are used. A **ledger line** is simply an extension of the staff.

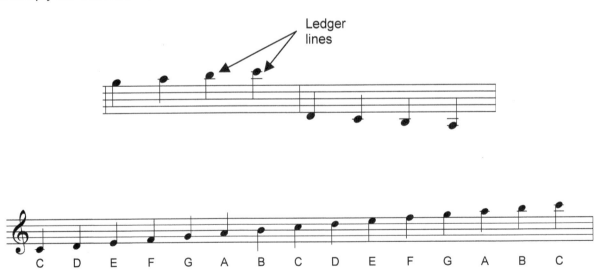

Parts of a Note

Notes may or may not have stems. Their note heads may be filled in, or the note will simply consist of an unfilled note head. These different characteristics are used to indicate the time value of a note. Chapter 6 will examine the notation of rhythm. When stems are added to notes, it is important that they are written in the correct direction. Notes above the middle line usually have their stems all written downward on the left of the note head. Notes that are below the middle line should have their stems written in an upward direction with their stems on the right side. A note found on the middle line can have its stem go in either direction. Flags are always added to the right side of the note.

When notes are joined, the stems will take the direction of the note that is the greatest distance from the middle line of the staff.

Understanding Sharps(♯) and Flats (♭)

The smallest standard distance between any two given notes in the West, is the **semitone**. The semitone can be found between any two adjacent keys on the piano. In other words, take any key on the piano and go to the note immediately above or below it. The **whole tone** is the distance of two semitones. On the guitar, the distance of one fret is a semitone or a **half step**. A **whole tone** or **tone** is the distance of two frets.

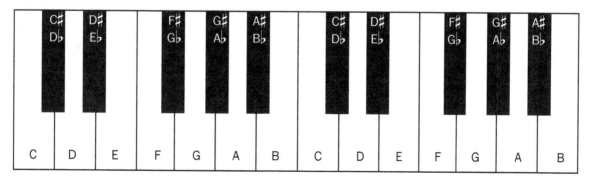

A **sharp** (♯) raises a note by one semitone (one fret).

A **flat** (♭) lowers a note by one semitone (one fret).

A **natural** (♮) cancels the previous sharp or flat and returns the note to its original pitch.

A **double sharp** (x) raises a natural note by two semitones (two frets).

A double sharp (**x**) raises a sharp by one semitone (one fret)

A **double flat** (♭♭) lowers a natural note by two semitones (two frets).

A double flat (♭♭) lowers a flat by one semitone (one fret).

- If you raise a natural note (♮) by one semitone, the note will become a sharp. A natural note is a note that is not sharp or flat.
- If you lower a natural note one semitone, it will become a flat.
- By raising a flat (♭) one semitone, you obtain a natural note.
- Lowering a sharp (♯) one semitone, will give you a natural note.

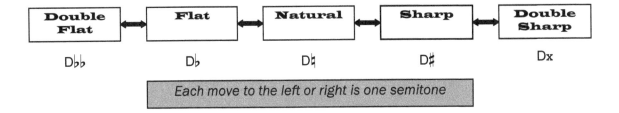

For example:
- If you raise an F one semitone, it becomes an F♯.
- If you raise a D♭ one semitone, it becomes a D♮.
- If you lower a G one semitone, it becomes a G♭.
- If you lower a G♯ one semitone, it becomes a G♮.
- If you lower an A♭ one semitone, it becomes an A♭♭.
- If you raise a G♯ one semitone, it becomes a Gx.

Enharmonic Equivalents

Enharmonic equivalents are notes that sound the same but are written with different letter-names. For example, the F♯ and G♭ are both found on the 2nd fret of the sixth string and sound identical. G♯ and A♭ both share the 1st fret of the third string. Context determines whether a note should be called an F♯ or a G♭. Here are some other notes you should know about:

B♯ = C   E♯ = F   F♭ = E   C♭ = B

When you see a sharp or flat between the treble clef and the time signature, the sharp(s) or flat(s) effect the music from that point forward. The collection of sharps or flats is called a **key signature**. In the following example, all of the F's are sharp. The F♯ found in the key signature effects all F♯'s regardless of octave. A more detailed discussion of key signatures is found in chapter 2.

Sharps or flats that are not part of the key signature (called **accidentals**) effect only the measure in which they appear. The next bar line cancels out all previous sharps or flats that are not part of the key signature. A natural sign cancels out an accidental for the remainder of the measure.

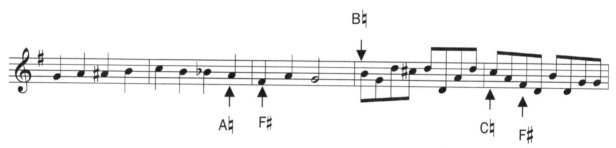

Understanding Sharps (♯) and Flats (♭) on the Guitar

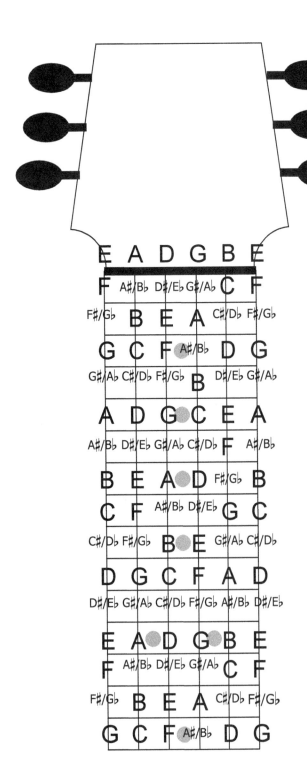

Tip 1: The grid on the left shows the letter-names of the notes on the guitar. The quickest way to learn these notes is to memorize the location of the natural notes. Once you know the location of the natural notes, you can very easily determine the location of any sharps or flats. Notice how E—F, and B—C are adjacent to one another (i.e., no frets between them), the rest of the natural notes have one fret between them.

Tip 2: The most efficient way to learn the fretboard is to take a string each week and memorize the location of the natural notes. The first 3 days of the week should be spent moving up and down the sixth string, naming the notes as you land on them. The next four days should be spent picking random notes on the neck. Identify each note as quickly as possible. Repeat this procedure for the remaining strings.

Tip 3: The notes on the 12th fret have the same letter-names as the open strings. The notes above the 12th fret repeat, so once you learn the notes up to the 12th fret, you will already know the notes found on the remaining frets. You should also notice that the notes on the 6th and 1st strings have identical letter-names.

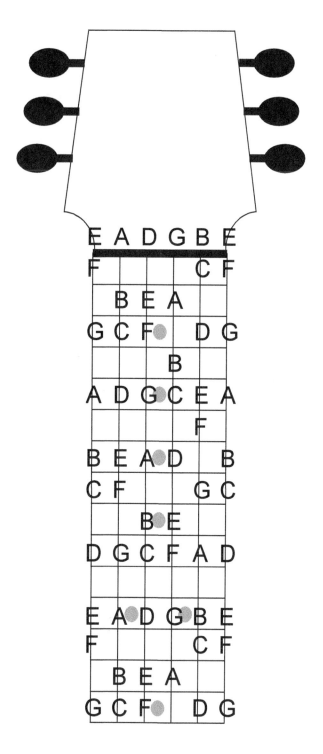

The importance of learning the fretboard cannot be over emphasized. In order to understand music theory you must know the fretboard. Set aside some time each day to work on this task. You need to be able to instantly identify any note on the guitar.

Exercises

1. On the following neck diagrams, locate and write out the following notes:

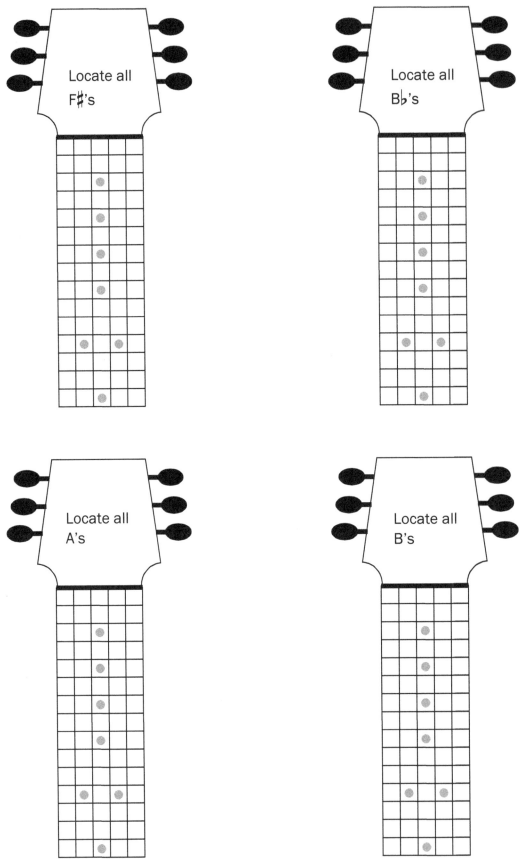

Absolute Essentials of Music Theory for Guitar

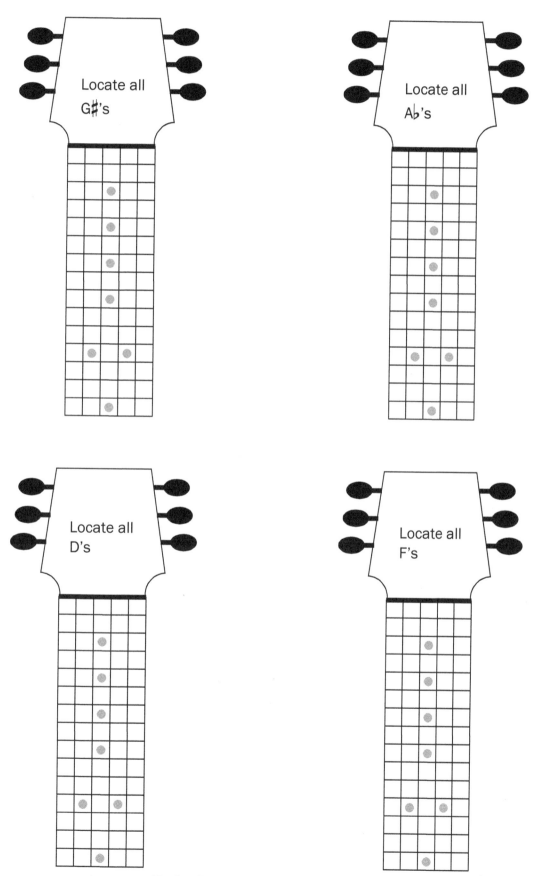

2. Identify the following notes.

3. Write enharmonic equivalents for the following notes:

a) E♭
b) G♯
c) F♯
d) B♯
e) C♭
f) F♭
g) A♯

4. Semitones and whole tones.

    a) If you raise a G♭ one semitone you have _____
    b) If you raise a B one whole tone you have _____
    c) If you raise an A one semitone you have _____
    d) If you raise a C♯ one whole tone you have _____
    e) If you lower a G♭ one semitone you have _____
    f) If you lower an F one whole tone you have _____
    g) If you lower a D♭ one semitone you have _____

Answers

1. On the following neck diagrams, locate and write out the following notes:

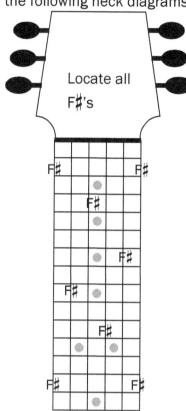

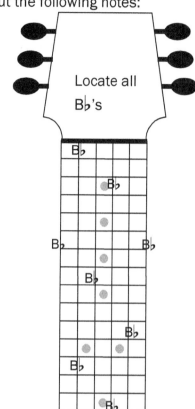

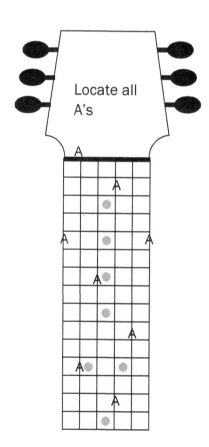

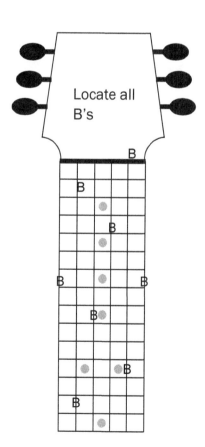

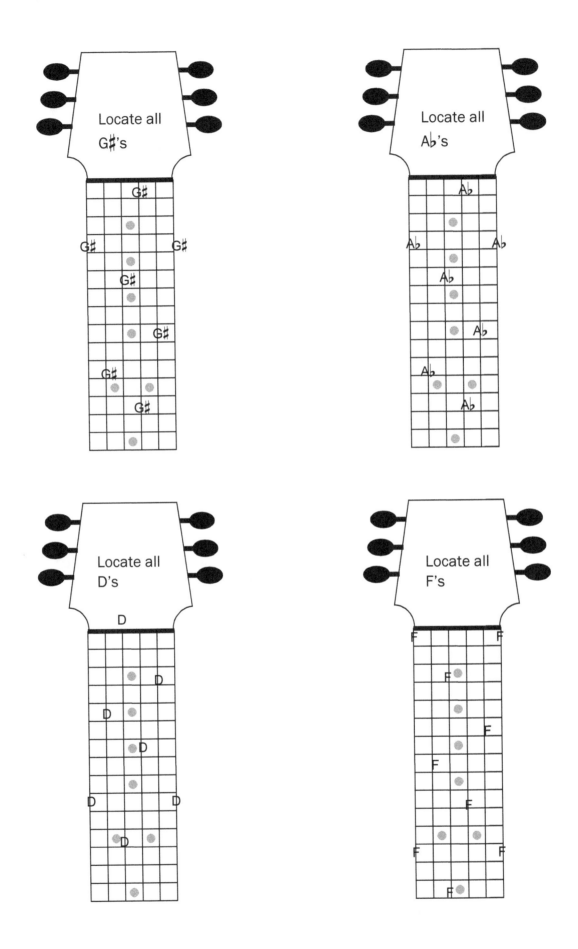

Absolute Essentials of Music Theory for Guitar

2.

| B | B | G | B♭ | G | G | F | G♭ | C | C | G | D♯ | G♭ | D♯ | A |

| A | F♯ | B | E | B | D | E | D♯ | C | E | D | E | A | A♯ | D |

| A | D | C | G | C | B | D | B | D | A | B♯ | B♭ | C | F | B♮ |

In the first measure above, the third last note is a G♭ not a G. This is because a G♭ was introduced earlier in the measure. Remember that accidentals effect any additional occurrences of the note in the measure. The bar line cancels out accidentals.

2. Write enharmonic equivalents for the following notes:

h) E♭ ⇔ D♯

i) G♯ ⇔ A♭

j) F♯ ⇔ G♭

k) B♯ ⇔ C

l) C♭ ⇔ B

m) F♭ ⇔ E

n) A♯ ⇔ B♭

3. Semitones and whole tones.

h)   If you raise a G♭ one semitone you have _____ G♮

i)   If you raise a B one whole tone you have _____ C♯/D♭

j)   If you raise an A one semitone you have _____ A♯/B♭

k)   If you raise a C♯ one whole tone you have _____ D♯/E♭

l)   If you lower a G♭ one semitone you have _____ G♭♭/F

m)   If you lower an F one whole tone you have _____ E♭/D♯

n)   If you lower a D♭ one semitone you have _____ C/D♭♭

For each answer in this question, enharmonic equivalents are shown. Context will determine the "correct" answer. You will understand this after completing the chapters on intervals and chords.

Chapter 2

Scales

What are Scales?

The word scale comes from the Italian word *scala*, which means ladder. A **scale** is a collection of pitches that have been arranged into a specific ascending and descending order. Scales are used as a basis for composition or as a vehicle for improvisation.

The Major Scale

The *major scale* is often used for the derivation of many of the theoretical principles of Western music theory and also happens to be the most common scale in popular music. Consequently, this will be the first scale to be examined.

In order to have a *major scale*, there must be a specific arrangement of semitones and whole tones. The C major scale consists of the following notes:

C D E F G A B C

T = Whole Tone: A whole tone is the distance of two semitones. The whole tone is also called a *tone* or a *whole step*.

ST = Semitone: The semitone is also known as a *half step*.

C (T) D (T) E (ST) F (T) G (T) A (T) B (ST) C

To build any major scale simply proceed through the following progression of semitones and whole tones:

Major Scale Formula: T T ST T T T ST

If you follow this formula starting with any note other than C, you will find that you are required to use sharps or flats. Here is a list of all of the major scales.

C major	C D E F G A B C
G major	G A B C D E F♯ G
D major	D E F♯ G A B C♯ D
A major	A B C♯ D E F♯ G♯ A
E major	E F♯ G♯ A B C♯ D♯ E
B major	B C♯ D♯ E F♯ G♯ A♯ B
F♯ major	F♯ G♯ A♯ B C♯ D♯ E♯ F♯
C♯ major	C♯ D♯ E♯ F♯ G♯ A♯ B♯ C♯

F major	F G A B♭ C D E F
B♭ major	B♭ C D E♭ F G A B♭
E♭ major	E♭ F G A♭ B♭ C D E♭
A♭ major	A♭ B♭ C D♭ E♭ F G A♭
D♭ major	D♭ E♭ F G♭ A♭ B♭ C D♭
G♭ major	G♭ A♭ B♭ C♭ D♭ E♭ F G♭
C♭ major	C♭ D♭ E♭ F♭ G♭ A♭ B♭ C♭

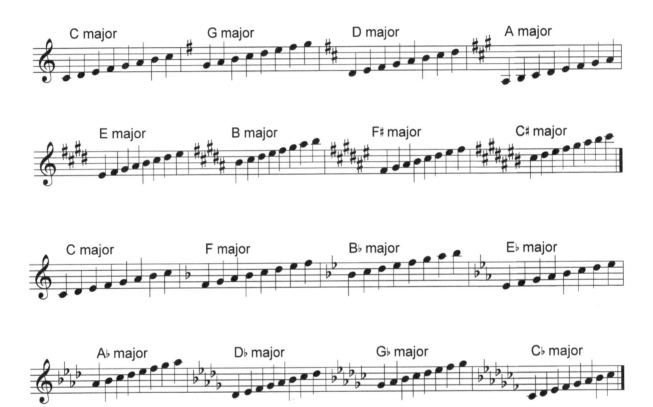

Key Signatures

Sharps and flats are written on the staff in a specific order and are collectively called a **key signature**. This standardization means that when you see one sharp, you will be in the key of G major and the one sharp, will be the F♯. If you see three flats, you would be in the key of E♭. The exceptions to this will be discussed later.

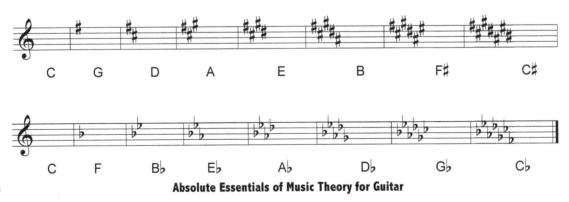

There are a total of 15 major scales. However, of these 15 scales, only 12 actually sound different. When you were introduced to the sharps and flats in Chapter 1, you were introduced to the concept of **enharmonic equivalents**. The C♭ major scale sounds identical to the B major scale; the G♭ major scale sounds the same as the F♯ major scale; and the D♭ major scale has the same sound as the C♯ major scale. Context will determine the most appropriate scale choice. If a composition is in the key of B major and **modulates** (changes keys) to F♯ major, it would be most logical to write the composition in F♯ major instead G♭ major. The reason is quite simple, moving from B to F♯ major would mean moving from five to six sharps. If you were to go from B to G♭, you would have to cancel out the five sharps in the B major scale and introduce 6 flats. There are other theoretical reasons why you would favor one key over the other on paper, but they do not concern us here.

The easiest way to learn the notes in each major scale is to memorize the following:

C major	No sharps or flats
G major	One sharp
D major	Two sharps
A major	Three sharps
E major	Four sharps
B major	Five sharps
F♯ major	Six sharps
C♯ major	Seven sharps
F major	One flat
B♭ major	Two flats
E♭ major	Three flats
A♭ major	Four flats
D♭ major	Five flats
G♭ major	Six flats
C♭ major	Seven flats

Take note of the number of sharps or flats contained in each scale. A great way to memorize the major scales is to first memorize:

C major has no sharps or flats;
C♯ major has every note sharp; and
C♭ major has every note flat.

Now take the remaining scales and pair them up. Take each pair of scales and spend a little time each day repeating the number of sharps or flats that occur in the scale. It is best to recite the notes in each scale ascending and descending. For example, on day one, you would repeat that G major has one sharp (F♯) and D major has two sharps (F♯ and C♯). The notes in each of these ascending and descending scales are:

G major: G A B C D E F♯ G; G F♯ E D C B A G

D major: D E F♯ G A B C♯ D; D C♯ B A G F♯ E D

Repeat the notes in the scales throughout the day. On the next day, you would memorize that A major has three sharps and E major has four sharps. You should also repeat all of the scales you memorized over the previous day(s). Do this with the remaining scales and you will learn all of the major scales and their notes in just six days.

Below, you will find a mnemonic that will help you learn the sharps and flats. The first letter of each word represents the note(s) that is/are sharp in the key. G major has one sharp and the one sharp is F♯ (Father). D major has two sharps and the sharps are F♯ and C♯ (Father Charles). B major has five sharps: F♯, C♯, G♯, D♯ and A♯ (Father Charles Goes Down And). As you can see, the sharps are cumulative when presented in the order shown.

Sharps
Father Charles Goes Down And Ends Battle

In all key signatures, you will find each note that is to be sharp or flat, is indicated only once on the staff. For example, in A major there are three sharps, F♯, C♯ and G♯. On the staff, you will notice that these sharps are only indicated in one octave. When a note is marked as sharp or flat by a key signature, it means that all like notes are sharp or flat as well. The following example demonstrates this concept.

All of the F's, C's and G's are sharp in A major:

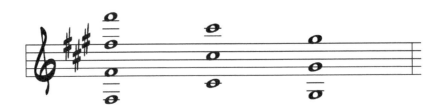

Unless a song changes keys, the key signature found at the beginning of a piece of music indicates that the entire piece is in a certain key. A change of key, or **modulation** as it is more formally known, would be indicated by introducing a new key signature.

To memorize the order that flats appear in a key signature, you can reuse the mnemonic device introduced for the sharps. For the flats, it is simply read backwards:

Flats
Battle Ends And Down Goes Charles Father

Absolute Essentials of Music Theory for Guitar

B♭ major has two flats: B♭ and E♭ (**B**attle **E**nds). A♭ major has four flats: B♭, E♭, A♭ and D♭ (**B**attle **E**nds **A**nd **D**own).

Application

Now that you understand how major scales are built, it is time to apply them to the guitar. The most efficient way to play scales is to use moveable scale forms. Moveable scales are as their name implies—moveable. This means that you can take one scale shape and move it up or down the neck of the guitar to produce any desired scale. In other words, once you learn one of the moveable shapes for a major scale, you just have to move it up or down to produce the 11 other major scales.

Here is how it works. **The black notes in each scale form represent the root notes.** The root note indicates the letter-name of the scale. The scales shown in this book contain two or more root notes. To simplify things we will identify scale forms by the root note found on the lowest string of the scale. We will refer to either sixth, fifth, or fourth root scale forms. If we move the following 6th root major scale form so that the first finger is on the 8th fret you will have a C major scale.

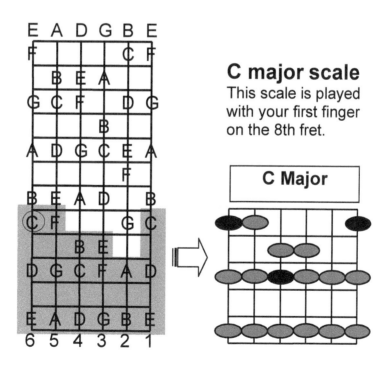

C major scale
This scale is played with your first finger on the 8th fret.

Now move this same scale shape so that the sixth root is on the first fret. Since the root note is on the note F, we now have an F major scale.

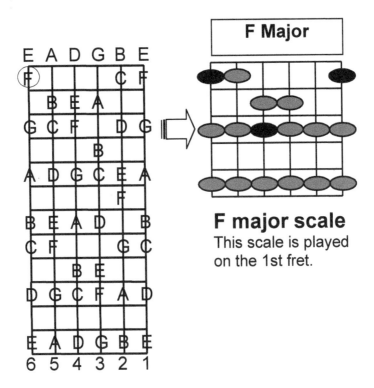

F major scale
This scale is played on the 1st fret.

As an additional example, consider what happens if we move this major scale up to the 4th fret. We will now have an A♭ major scale. This scale could also be called a G♯ major scale. This is due to the fact that A♭ and G♯ are both played on the same fret. These notes are referred to as *enharmonic equivalents*—they sound the same but are called two different things. A♭ is more common than G♯ major simply due to the letter-names of each scale. The A♭ major scale contains A♭-B♭-C-D♭-E♭-F-G-A♭, while the G♯ major scale is comprised of G♯-A♯-B♯-C♯-D♯-E♯-Fx-G♯.

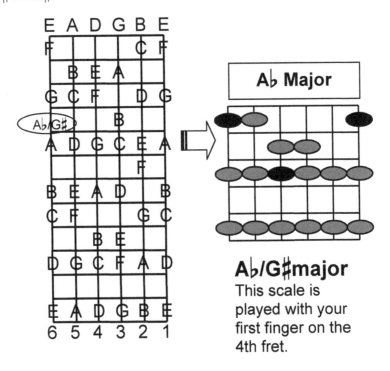

A♭/G♯ major
This scale is played with your first finger on the 4th fret.

We will now look at the most common fingerings for the major scale. First we will examine C major. After, we will examine the fingerings for the F major scale. Since there are seven different notes in the major scale you will find one fingering that commences on each note of the scale.

The Major Scale

Formula:

1	2	3	4	5	6	7	T T ST T T T ST
C	D	E	F	G	A	B	

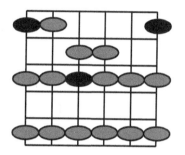

This scale form begins on the first note of the major scale.

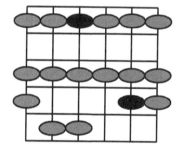

This scale form begins on the second note of the major scale.

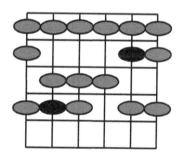

This scale form begins on the third note of the major scale.

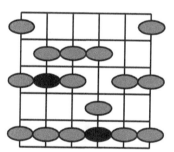

This scale form begins on the fourth note of the major scale.

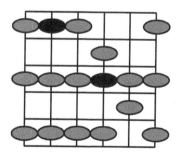

This scale form begins on the fifth note of the major scale.

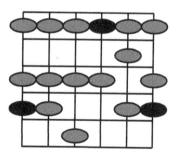

This scale form begins on the sixth note of the major scale.

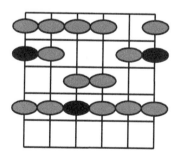

This scale form begins on the seventh note of the major scale.

If we position the seven fingerings for the major scale so that the root notes are on C's, we will have:

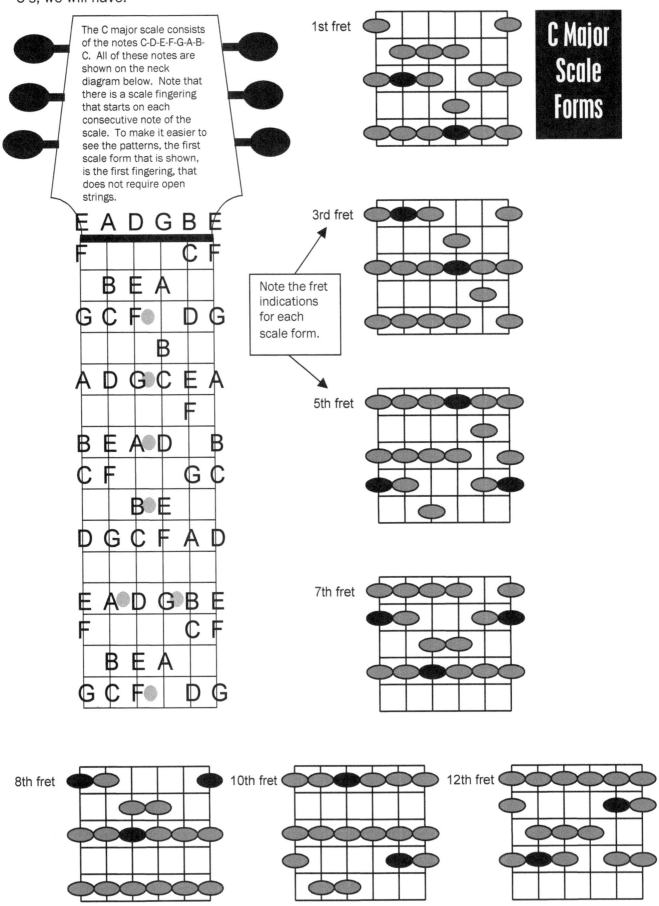

The C major scale consists of the notes C-D-E-F-G-A-B-C. All of these notes are shown on the neck diagram below. Note that there is a scale fingering that starts on each consecutive note of the scale. To make it easier to see the patterns, the first scale form that is shown, is the first fingering, that does not require open strings.

C Major Scale Forms

1st fret

3rd fret

Note the fret indications for each scale form.

5th fret

7th fret

8th fret

10th fret

12th fret

Absolute Essentials of Music Theory for Guitar

We will now look at the seven scale forms for F major.

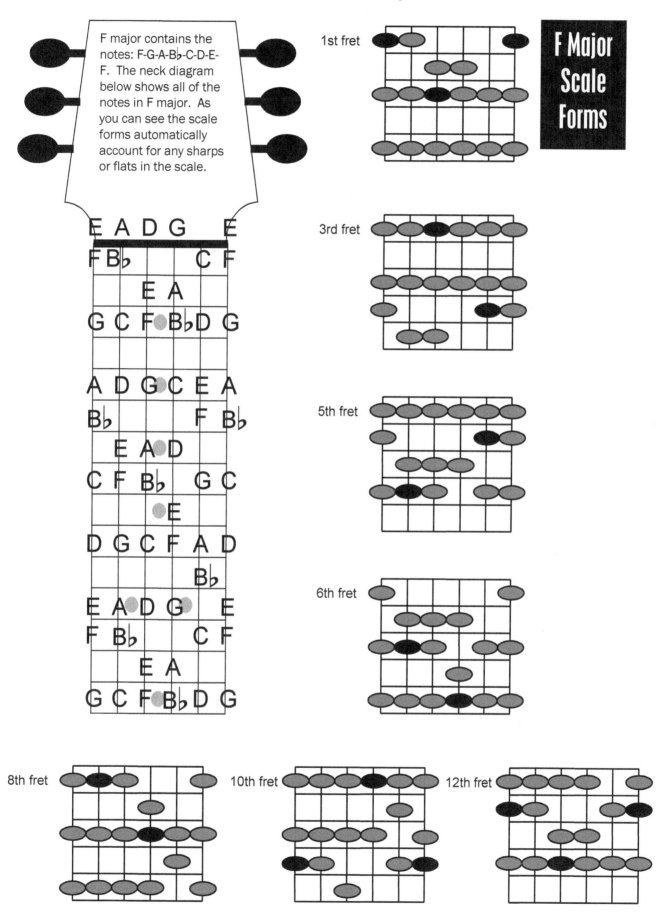

F major contains the notes: F-G-A-B♭-C-D-E-F. The neck diagram below shows all of the notes in F major. As you can see the scale forms automatically account for any sharps or flats in the scale.

F Major Scale Forms

1st fret

3rd fret

5th fret

6th fret

8th fret

10th fret

12th fret

Major Scale

There are no fret indications shown for the major scale forms, since they can be performed on any fret. Move each scale form so that the root notes are on the appropriate notes for the desired scale.

Formula:

1	2	3	4	5	6	7
C	D	E	F	G	A	B

T T ST T T T ST

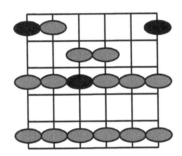

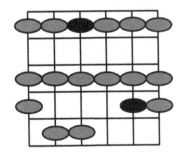

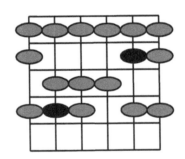

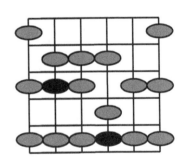

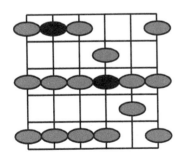

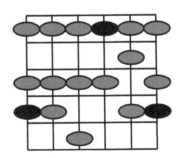

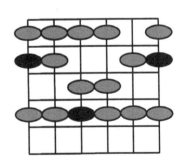

Absolute Essentials of Music Theory for Guitar

Minor Scales

Minor scales are used in most styles of music and are second in popularity to the major scale. Minor scales do not have their own unique key signatures but borrow from what is referred to as their **relative major scale**. To build a minor scale, go to the VI degree of the major scale and re-write the scale (including any sharps or flats) commencing on this sixth note. Roman numerals are often used to notate scale degrees.

C major

C   D   E   F   G   A   B   C

⇑

VI

A minor

A   B   C   D   E   F   G   A

Table of Natural Minor Scales

A minor:	A B C D E F G A
E minor:	E F♯ G A B C D E
B minor:	B C♯ D E F♯ G A B
F♯ minor:	F♯ G♯ A B C♯ D E F♯
C♯ minor:	C♯ D♯ E F♯ G♯ A B C♯
G♯ minor:	G♯ A♯ B C♯ D♯ E F♯ G♯
D♯ minor:	D♯ E♯ F♯ G♯ A♯ B C♯ D♯
A♯ minor:	A♯ B♯ C♯ D♯ E♯ F♯ G♯ A♯
D minor:	D E F G A B♭ C D
G minor:	G A B♭ C D E♭ F G
C minor:	C D E♭ F G A♭ B♭ C
F minor:	F G A♭ B♭ C D♭ E♭ F
B♭ minor:	B♭ C D♭ E♭ F G♭ A♭ B♭
E♭ minor:	E♭ F G♭ A♭ B♭ C♭ D♭ E♭
A♭ minor:	A♭ B♭ C♭ D♭ E♭ F♭ G♭ A♭

Natural Minor

Table of Relative Minor Scales

C major	C D E F G A B C
A minor	A B C D E F G A
G major	G A B C D E F♯ G
E minor	E F♯ G A B C D E
D major	D E F♯ G A B C♯ D
B minor	B C♯ D E F♯ G A B
A major	A B C♯ D E F♯ G♯ A
F♯ minor	F♯ G♯ A B C♯ D E F♯
E major	E F♯ G♯ A B C♯ D♯ E
C♯ minor	C♯ D♯ E F♯ G♯ A B C♯
B major	B C♯ D♯ E F♯ G♯ A♯ B
G♯ minor	G♯ A♯ B C♯ D♯ E F♯ G♯

Absolute Essentials of Music Theory for Guitar

F♯ major	F♯ G♯ A♯ B C♯ D♯ E♯ F♯
D♯ minor	D♯ E♯ F♯ G♯ A♯ B C♯ D♯

C♯ major	C♯ D♯ E♯ F♯ G♯ A♯ B♯ C♯
A♯ minor	A♯ B♯ C♯ D♯ E♯ F♯ G♯ A♯

F major	F G A B♭ C D E F
D minor	D E F G A B♭ C D

B♭ major	B♭ C D E♭ F G A B♭
G minor	G A B♭ C D E♭ F G

E♭ major	E♭ F G A♭ B♭ C D E♭
C minor	C D E♭ F G A♭ B♭ C

A♭ major	A♭ B♭ C D♭ E♭ F G A♭
F minor	F G A♭ B♭ C D♭ E♭ F

D♭ major	D♭ E♭ F G♭ A♭ B♭ C D♭
B♭ minor	B♭ C D♭ E♭ F G♭ A♭ B♭

G♭ major	G♭ A♭ B♭ C♭ D♭ E♭ F G♭
E♭ minor	E♭ F G♭ A♭ B♭ C♭ D♭ E♭

C♭ major	C♭ D♭ E♭ F♭ G♭ A♭ B♭ C♭
A♭ minor	A♭ B♭ C♭ D♭ E♭ F♭ G♭ A♭

Below you will see the key signatures for each minor scale.

Am   Em   Bm   F♯m   C♯m   G♯m   D♯m   A♯m

Am   Dm   Gm   Cm   Fm   B♭m   E♭m   A♭m

Absolute Essentials of Music Theory for Guitar

Minor Scale

Formula:

1	2	♭3	4	5	♭6	♭7
C	D	E♭	F	G	A♭	B♭

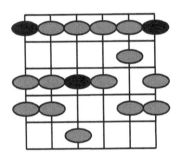

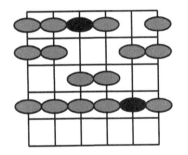

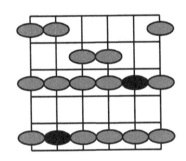

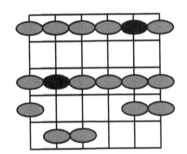

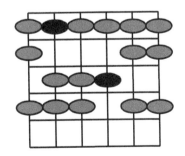

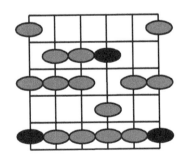

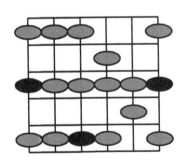

Absolute Essentials of Music Theory for Guitar

Harmonic Minor Scale

To build a **harmonic minor scale**, raise the VII degree of the minor scale.

A minor:

A harmonic minor:

Harmonic Minor

Absolute Essentials of Music Theory for Guitar

Harmonic Minor Scale

Formula:

1	2	b3	4	5	b6	7
C	D	Eb	F	G	Ab	B

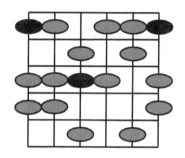

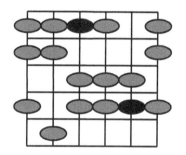

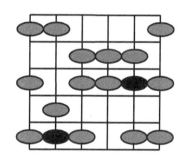

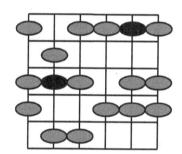

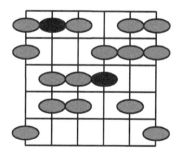

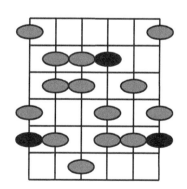

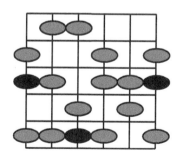

Melodic Minor Scale

To build a **melodic minor scale**, raise the VI and VII degrees of the minor scale ascending and lower them descending.

A melodic minor ascending (raise VI & VII):

A   B   C   D   E   F♯   G♯   A
                        ⇑   ⇑
                        VI   VII

A melodic minor descending (lower VI & VII):

A   G♮   F♮   E   D   C   B   A
     ⇑   ⇑
     VII   VI

The melodic minor scale has a different ascending and descending form. The descending form is the same as the natural minor scale. For the purpose of improvisation, the ascending version will yield the most interesting possibilities. This ascending form is very common in jazz improvisation. When the melodic minor scale's ascending form (raised VI and VII) is used ascending and descending you have what is referred to as the *Jazz Minor* or the *Real Melodic Minor scale*.

A Jazz Minor:

A   B   C   D   E   F♯   G♯   A

You may also find it helpful to think of the Jazz Minor scale as being a major scale with a ♭3.

Melodic Minor Ascending   **Melodic Minor Descending**

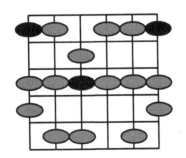   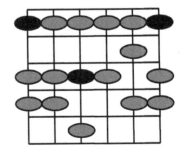

Melodic Minor

Jazz Minor Scale

Formula:

1	2	♭3	4	5	6	7
C	D	E♭	F	G	A	B

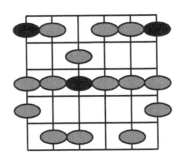

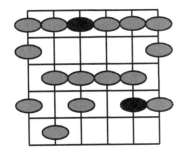
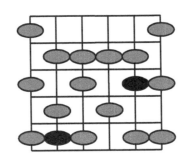
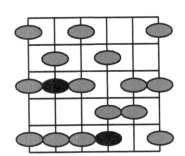

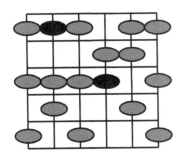
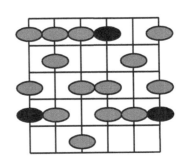
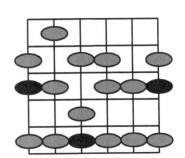

Pentatonic Scales

A pentatonic scale is a five note scale. There are many different types of pentatonic scales, but the most common are the major and minor pentatonic scales.

The major pentatonic scale is quite often derived by omitting the IV and VII degrees of the major scale. For example, to build a C major pentatonic scale you would drop the F and B from the C major scale.

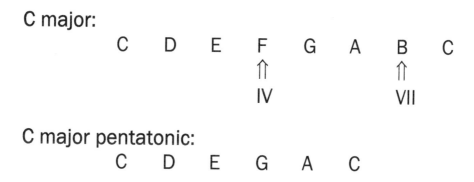

C major:

| C | D | E | F | G | A | B | C |

IV   VII

C major pentatonic:

C   D   E   G   A   C

The same procedure is often followed for the derivation of the minor pentatonic scale except this time the II and VI degrees are dropped from the minor scale:

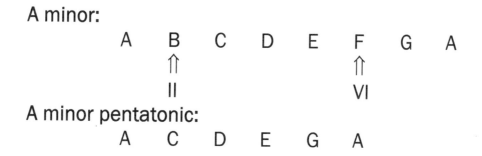

A minor:

A   B   C   D   E   F   G   A

II   VI

A minor pentatonic:

A   C   D   E   G   A

Major Pentatonic

C major pentatonic   G major pentatonic   D major pentatonic   A major pentatonic

E major pentatonic   B major pentatonic   F♯ major pentatonic   C♯ major pentatonic

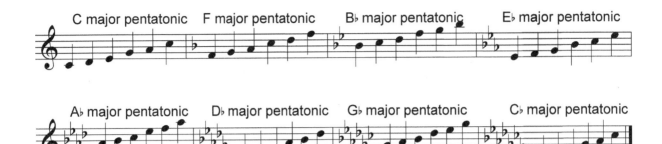

Minor Pentatonic

Absolute Essentials of Music Theory for Guitar

Major Pentatonic Scale

Formula:

1	2	3	5	6
C	D	E	G	A

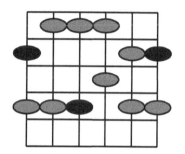

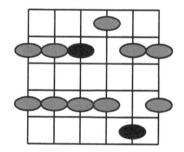

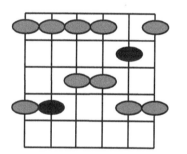

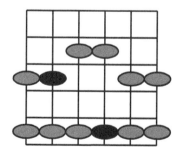

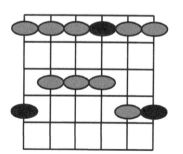

Minor Pentatonic Scale

Formula:

1	b3	4	5	b7
C	Eb	F	G	Bb

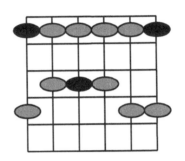

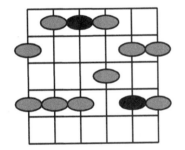

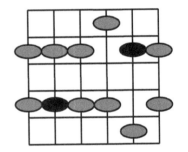

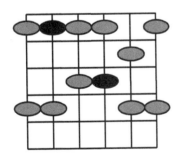

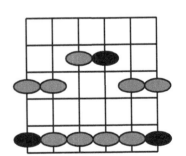

Absolute Essentials of Music Theory for Guitar

Exercises

1. Using letter-names, write the notes for the following scales:

   a) A major
   b) E minor
   c) G harmonic minor
   d) F♯ major
   e) D♭ major
   f) G melodic minor
   g) B pentatonic minor

2. In the treble clef, write the following scales with the appropriate key signatures.

   a) E major
   b) A♭ major
   c) C♯ harmonic minor
   d) F melodic minor
   e) F minor pentatonic
   f) G melodic minor

3. What is the relative minor or major scale for the following:

   a) G major
   b) D minor
   c) F♯ minor
   d) F♯ major

Answers

1. Using letter-names, write the notes for the following scales:

   a) A major
      A B C♯ D E F♯ G♯

   b) E minor
      E F♯ G A B C D

   c) G harmonic minor
      G A B♭ C D E♭ F♯

   d) F♯ major
      F♯ G♯ A♯ B C♯ D♯ E♯

   e) D♭ major
      D♭ E♭ F G♭ A♭ B♭ C

   f) G melodic minor
      G A B♭ C D E♮ F♯ G F♮ E♭ D C B♭ A G

   g) B pentatonic minor
      B D E F♯ A

2. In the treble clef, write the following scales with the appropriate key signatures.

E major

A♭ major

Absolute Essentials of Music Theory for Guitar

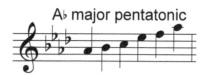
Ab major pentatonic

C♯ Harmonic Minor

F Melodic Minor

F minor pentatonic

G Melodic Minor

3. What is the relative minor or major scale for the following:
   a. G major ⇔ E minor
   b. D minor ⇔ F major
   c. F♯ minor ⇔ A major
   d. F♯ major ⇔ D♯ minor

Chapter 3

Intervals

Intervals

An **interval** is the distance between any two given notes. Notes that are played simultaneously are called **harmonic intervals**, while notes that are played in succession, are referred to as **melodic intervals**.

Harmonic intervals   Melodic intervals

To determine the size of an interval simply count from the lower note to the upper note of the interval. When counting up remember to count the starting note as the number one. For example, to determine the distance between the notes F and E you would arrive at the distance of a seventh.

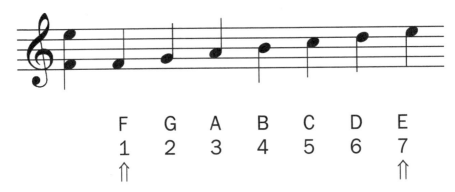

After determining the distance between the two notes you must next determine the interval's **quality**. You now compare the upper note to the major scale of the lower note. If the upper note is contained in the major scale of the lower note (i.e., if the E is contained in the F major scale in the above example), you have a **diatonic interval**.

The diatonic intervals of a major scale are: the *perfect unison, major second, major third, perfect fourth, perfect fifth, major sixth, major seventh* and the *perfect octave*.

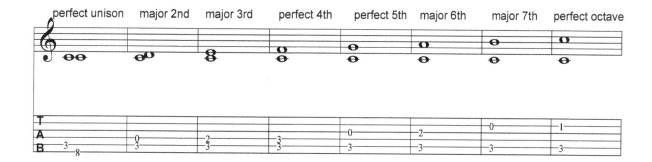

Interval Classification

The unison, 4th, 5th and the octave (8th) are considered to be *perfect intervals*. If a perfect interval is raised by one semitone, it becomes an *augmented interval*. A perfect interval lowered by one semitone will become a *diminished interval*.

Each move to the left or right represents the distance of one semitone.

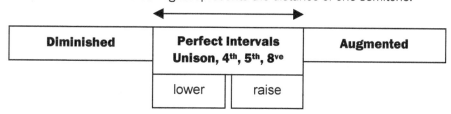

The remaining intervals, the second, third, sixth and the seventh, are considered to be *major* intervals if the upper note of the interval is contained in the major scale of the lower note. A major interval, lowered by one semitone, becomes a *minor* interval. A lowered minor interval becomes a *diminished* interval. If a major interval is raised it will be called an *augmented* interval.

Each move to the left or right represents the distance of one semitone.

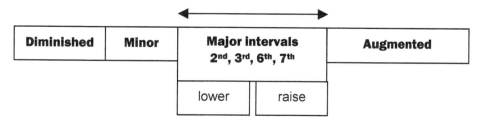

The preceding discussion of intervals dealt with **simple intervals**. A simple interval is an interval that is no larger than an octave. Any interval that is larger than an octave is deemed to be a **compound interval**. The most common compound intervals are the ninth, eleventh and thirteenth.

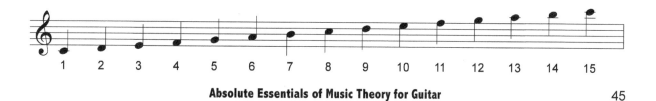

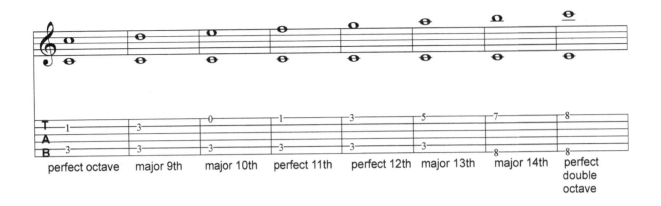

Compound intervals take on the same quality as their simple interval counterparts. A major second above C is the note D. A major 9th above C is also a D.

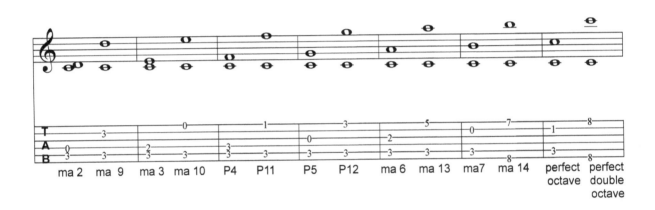

Just as you can have an aug 2nd, min 2nd, or a dim 2nd, you can therefore have an aug 9th, min 9th, or a dim 9th.

You can also have enharmonic intervals. The most common enharmonic equivalent intervals are:

aug 4 ⇔ dim 5
aug 2 ⇔ min 3
aug 6 ⇔ min 7
dim 7 ⇔ maj 6

Absolute Essentials of Music Theory for Guitar

Inverting Intervals

Simple intervals can be inverted. Inversion can be accomplished by either moving the bottom note of the interval up an octave, or by moving the top note of the interval down an octave.

When an interval is inverted you will find:

Perfect intervals remain **perfect**
Major intervals become **minor**
Minor intervals become **major**
Augmented intervals become **diminished**
Diminished intervals become **augmented**

To solve inverted intervals you can either count the actual distance between the notes, or you can subtract the interval from 9.

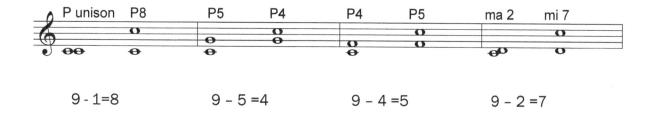

9 - 1=8   9 – 5 =4   9 – 4 =5   9 – 2 =7

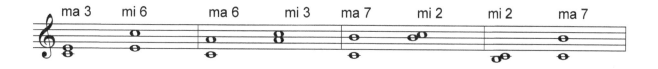

Application

A great way to practice scales is to use different intervallic combinations. The most common are thirds, fourths, fifths and sixths.

Thirds

The following pattern incorporates the interval of a third. For this pattern and the ones that follow, we will use the following major scale form:

C major

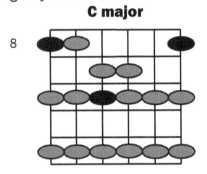

The above scale form is played on the eighth fret.

C major in thirds

Fourths

The major scale in fourths. This scale form is played on the eighth fret.

C major

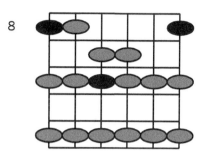

C major in fourths

Fifths

The major scale in fifths. This scale form is played on the eighth fret.

C major

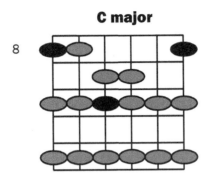

C major in fifths

Sixths

The major scale in sixths. This scale form is played on the eighth fret.

C major

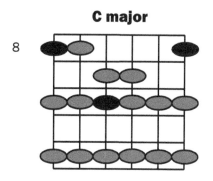

C major in sixths

Exercises

1. Identify the following intervals:

2. Identify the following intervals then invert and solve on the staff below.

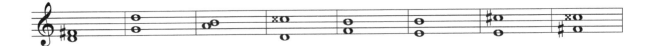

Absolute Essentials of Music Theory for Guitar

Answers

1.

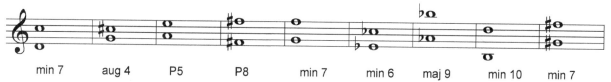

| min 7 | aug 4 | P5 | P8 | min 7 | min 6 | maj 9 | min 10 | min 7 |

The G♯ to F♯ interval found in the last measure of question 1 is a bit tricky. To solve intervals you have been told to go to the major scale of the bottom note of the interval. If you review the major scales found in chapter 2 you will find that there is no listing for G♯ major. Here is how you can solve this interval:

The notes in a G major scale are:

G major
G A B C D E F♯ G

Therefore to derive the notes in G♯, you simply raise every note in the G major scale by one semitone. The result is:

G♯ major
G♯ A♯ B♯ C♯ D♯ E♯ Fx G♯

Now that we have the G♯ major scale you can see that the F would have to be an Fx to be a major seventh. The interval is therefore a minor 7th.

2.

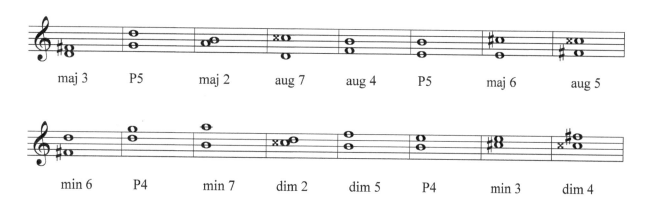

| maj 3 | P5 | maj 2 | aug 7 | aug 4 | P5 | maj 6 | aug 5 |

| min 6 | P4 | min 7 | dim 2 | dim 5 | P4 | min 3 | dim 4 |

Chapter 4

Chords

A **chord** is three or more notes played simultaneously. Chords provide accompaniment and support for melodies. There are many different types of chords, the most common are called triads.

Triads

A **triad** (Gr. *trias*, meaning a group of three) is a chord that contains three different notes. To understand how chords are built, we must return to the major scale. Take the first, third and fifth notes from the C major scale and you will have a C major chord.

How to Build any Triad

Step 1   Look at the appropriate formula for the chord you want.

Step 2   Go to the major scale of the chord. It does not matter whether you want a D♭ major triad or a D♭ diminished chord, you would still go to the D♭ major scale and select the appropriate notes.

Step 3   Extract the appropriate notes from the formula.

Step 4   Alter any necessary notes to fit the formula.

The flat (♭) symbol means to lower a note by a semitone while the sharp (♯) symbol indicates that the note must be raised by one semitone. As you extract the notes from the major scale be sure to remember the notes that are sharp or flat. If a note is already sharp in the major scale and must be lowered to follow a chord formula, it will become a natural note (♮). The figure below denotes the possible alterations.

Double Flat (♭♭)	Flat (♭)	Natural (♮)		Sharp (♯)	Double Sharp (x)
		lower	raise		
D♭♭	D♭	D		D♯	Dx

(Each move to the left or right represents the distance of a semitone.)

Major	1 3 5
Minor	1 ♭3 5
Diminished	1 ♭3 ♭5
Augmented	1 3 ♯5
Suspended 4	1 4 5
Suspended 2	1 2 5
Flat 5 (♭5)	1 3 ♭5

Example 1. G major: Formula ⇒ 1 3 5

Take the first, third and fifth notes out of the G major scale.

G major:

G	A	B	C	D	E	F♯	G
1	2	3	4	5	6	7	8
⇑		⇑		⇑			

For a major chord, you simply extract the first, third and fifth notes from the major scale. Therefore the notes in a G major chord are:

G	B	D
1	3	5

Example 2. D minor: Formula ⇒ 1 ♭3 5

Take the first, third and fifth notes out of the D major scale.

D major:

D	E	F♯	G	A	B	C♯	D
1	2	3	4	5	6	7	8
⇑		⇑		⇑			

For a minor chord, you must lower the third. The F♯ will become an F♮.
Therefore the notes in a D minor chord are:

$$D \quad F♮ \quad A$$
$$1 \quad ♭3 \quad 5$$

Example 3. A♭ diminished: Formula ⇒ 1 ♭3 ♭5
Take the first, third and fifth notes out of an A♭ major scale.

A♭ major:

$$A♭ \quad B♭ \quad C \quad D♭ \quad E♭ \quad F \quad G \quad A♭$$
$$1 \quad 2 \quad 3 \quad 4 \quad 5 \quad 6 \quad 7 \quad 8$$
$$⇑ \qquad\quad ⇑ \qquad\quad ⇑$$

For a diminished chord, you must lower the third and fifth notes from the
major scale. The C will become an C♭ and the E♭ will become an E♭♭.
Therefore the notes in an A♭ diminished chord are:

$$A♭ \quad C♭ \quad E♭♭$$
$$1 \quad ♭3 \quad ♭5$$

Example 4. F♯ augmented: Formula ⇒ 1 3 ♯5
Take the first, third and fifth notes out of the F♯ major scale.

F♯ major:

$$F♯ \quad G♯ \quad A♯ \quad B \quad C♯ \quad D♯ \quad E♯ \quad F♯$$
$$1 \quad 2 \quad 3 \quad 4 \quad 5 \quad 6 \quad 7 \quad 8$$
$$⇑ \qquad\quad ⇑ \qquad\quad ⇑$$

For an augmented chord extract the first, third and fifth notes from the major
scale and raise the 5th by one semitone. The C♯ will become a Cx. Therefore
the notes in an F♯ augmented chord are:

$$F♯ \quad A♯ \quad Cx$$
$$1 \quad 3 \quad ♯5$$

Example 5. F suspended 4: Formula ⇒ 1 4 5

Take the first, fourth and fifth notes out of the F major scale.

F major:

F	G	A	Bb	C	D	E	F
1	2	3	4	5	6	7	8
⇑			⇑	⇑			

For a suspended 4 chord, you simply extract the first, fourth and fifth notes from the major scale. Therefore the notes in an F sus 4 chord are:

F	Bb	C
1	4	5

Example 6. Ab suspended 2: Formula ⇒ 1 2 5

Take the first, second and fifth notes out of an Ab major scale.

Ab major:

Ab	Bb	C	Db	Eb	F	G	Ab
1	2	3	4	5	6	7	8
⇑	⇑			⇑			

For a suspended 2 chord extract the first, second and fifth notes from the major scale. Therefore the notes in an Ab sus 2 chord are:

Ab	Bb	Eb
1	2	5

Example 7. Ab b5: Formula ⇒ 1 3 b5

Take the first, third and fifth notes out of an Ab major scale.

Ab major:

Ab	Bb	C	Db	Eb	F	G	Ab
1	2	3	4	5	6	7	8
⇑		⇑		⇑			

For a ♭5 chord extract the first, third and lower the fifth from the major scale. Therefore the notes in an A♭ ♭5 chord are:

$$\begin{array}{ccc} A\flat & C & E\flat\flat \\ 1 & 3 & \flat5 \end{array}$$

As you can see from the formulas, three notes are necessary to form a triad. Often you will find one or more notes doubled in a triad. This is done to create a "bigger" sound or for smooth voice-leading. Voice-leading is the practice of connecting the notes from chord to chord in a smooth fashion. This is covered in the study of harmony.

Chord Sybolization

Just as there is no standardization of scale names from one region to another, there are many problems with the current system of identifying chords. The following abbreviations are frequently used:

maj ⇒ for major
min ⇒ for minor
dim ⇒ for diminished
aug ⇒ for augmented
sus 4 ⇒ for suspended 4
sus 2 ⇒ for suspended 2

Often, the major chord will have no indication following its letter-name. For example, the chords C maj, F maj and G maj, may be written as C, F, G. Minor chords are often abbreviated as: "m", "mi", or a minus sign "−" is used. The diminished triad is sometimes symbolized as "min ♭5", or as "dim (triad)". Bear in mind that "dim" is sometimes used to represent a diminished 7th chord. The augmented chord, which is usually abbreviated as "aug", is sometimes symbolized with a plus sign "+". For example, G+ and A♭+, would both be augmented triads. You should note that the plus sign is used to represent the major chord in some texts that cover classical music theory. Below you will see a summary of the most common ways that basic triads are symbolized.

Triad	Common Symbols	Best
Major	C, C ma, C Maj, C maj, C major, C Major, C+	C, C ma, C maj, C Maj
Minor	C mi, C min, C minor, C-, C m,	C mi, C min
Diminished	C dim, Cᵒ, C (dim), C min ♭5, Cᵒ (no 7), Cᵒ (omit 7)	C min ♭5, C dim, C dim(triad)
Augmented	C+, C aug, C aug 5, C ♯5, C +5	C aug, C+

Be aware that the diminished triad is not as popular as the diminished 7th chord. There is in fact, a big difference in sound between these two chords. The diminished triad consists of 1-♭3-♭5, while the diminished 7th chord contains 1-♭3-♭5-♭♭7. Since the diminished 7th is

Absolute Essentials of Music Theory for Guitar

the most popular, it is often just abbreviated as "dim" and it is assumed that the performer will play the diminished 7th chord. This obviously creates a problem with symbolizing the diminished triad. You can now see why it best to symbolize the diminished triad as C dim (triad), or C min ♭5. In other words, it is best to be as explicit as possible when you symbolize this chord to avoid confusion.

Below you will find a basic voicing for each type of triad.

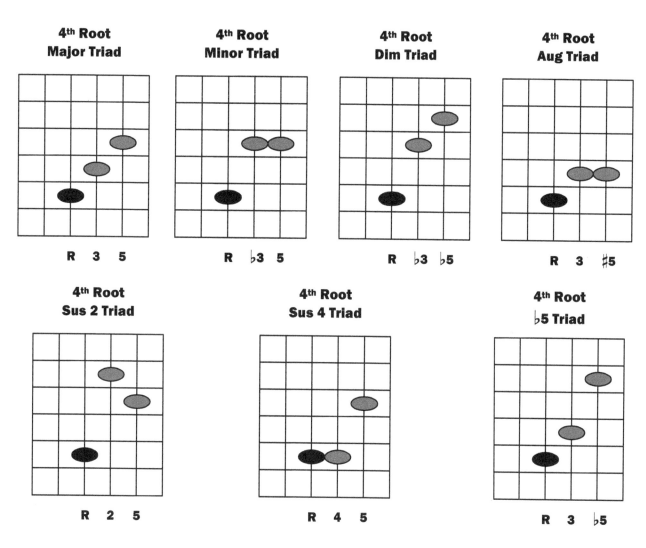

Triad Inversions

For variety and to allow for the smooth transition from one chord to the next, you will sometimes encounter inversions. In an inversion either the third or the fifth of the chord is the lowest sounding note of the chord.

Major

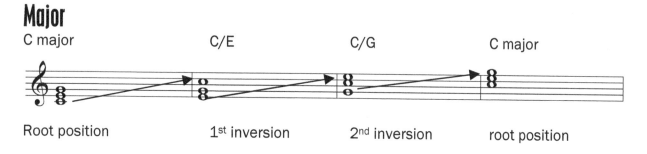

In root position the root (1) of the chord is the bass note. First inversion has the third in the bass and second inversion has the fifth in the bass. In modern notation you will see inversions notated as chord/bass note. For example, C/E means that you play a C major chord with E in the bass. A D/F♯ would mean that you play a D major chord and have F♯ as the lowest pitched note.

The most common triad inversions involve the standard triads: major, minor, diminished and augmented. The flat 5 triad and sus chords, are not usually inverted—when they are, their notation can become quite cumbersome.

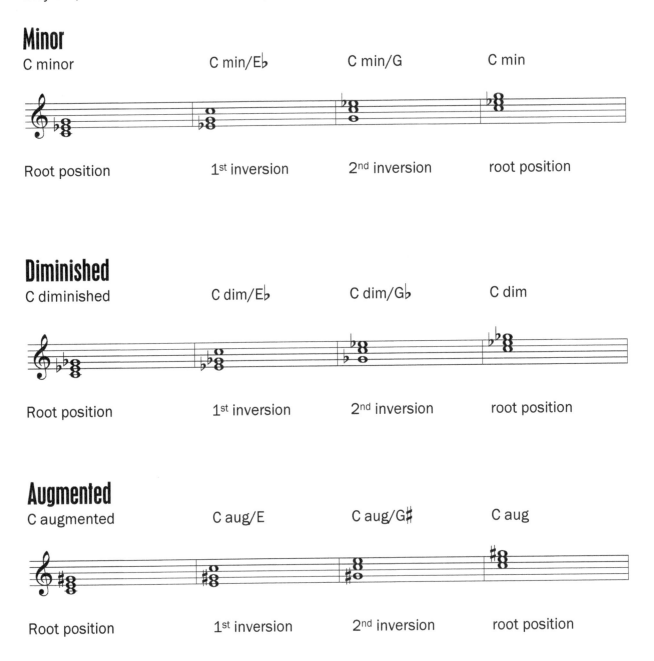

Minor

C minor   C min/E♭   C min/G   C min

Root position   1st inversion   2nd inversion   root position

Diminished

C diminished   C dim/E♭   C dim/G♭   C dim

Root position   1st inversion   2nd inversion   root position

Augmented

C augmented   C aug/E   C aug/G♯   C aug

Root position   1st inversion   2nd inversion   root position

   Absolute Essentials of Music Theory for Guitar

Triad Identification

To identify a triad you must first place the triad in root position. Chords are often written in **open position**—spread out over a distance greater than an octave. As you will recall, chords are built by stacking consecutive thirds (sus chords are an exception to this). This means that you should be able to write out the notes of a chord so that they appear on consecutive lines or spaces of the staff. When you have the notes written on consecutive lines or spaces of the staff, you have arranged the chord into **close position**. You can now determine the quality and inversion of the chord.

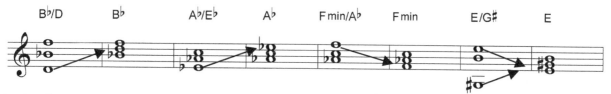

In the first measure shown above, you find the notes D-Bb-F. If you rearrange these notes so that they fall on consecutive lines or spaces, you end up with the Bb major chord shown in measure 2. Therefore, the chord in measure 1 is a Bb major chord with a D in the bass, i.e., 1st inversion. Follow the same procedure and you can solve the rest of the chords above.

Doubling

Chord tones may be doubled or even tripled. Although this has no effect on naming a chord, it does somewhat alter the sound of the chord. It is important to note that no matter how spread out a chord is, it is always the lowest note that determines a chord's position.

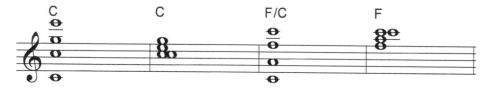

Application

Now that you know how basic chords are built, we will look at some examples of how to apply the formulas to actual chord fingerings.

First we will examine the C major triad:
Major chords are built by taking the 1st, 3rd and 5th notes from the major scale.

C Major Scale:	C	D	E	F	G	A	B
	1	2	3	4	5	6	7
	⇑		⇑		⇑		

The notes in a C major chord are C-E-G. To play the C major chord all you do is find the notes C-E-G on the fretboard. As you can see from the diagrams on the following page, there are many C's, E's and G's on the neck. You can play any combination of the notes C-E-G, and you will have a C major chord. You may double and even triple the notes as needed. Feel free to experiment and come up with multiple voicings for C major.

> This C major chord, has two C's, two E's and one G.

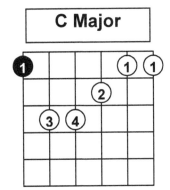

C Major

⇐ 8th fret ⇒

> The C major barre chord contains three C's, one E and two G's.

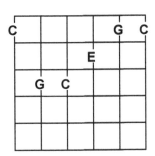

C Major Triads

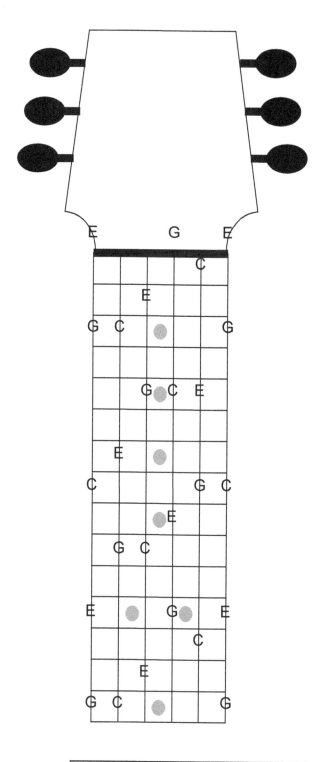

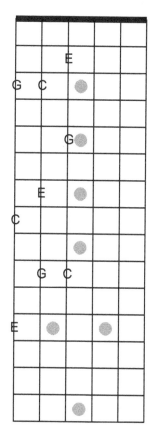

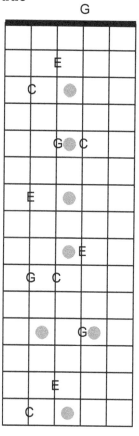

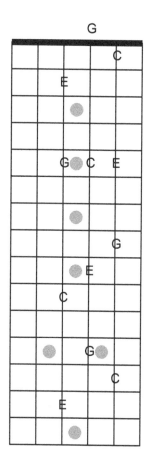

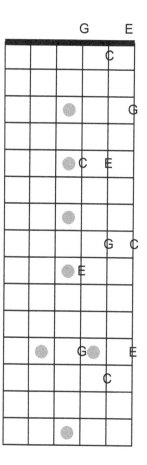

The C major triads found on the right show all of the inversions of C major on consecutive strings. To find ways to play any chord, draw a neck diagram with all of the chord tones. Once you have the neck diagram, you will see many possible ways to play the chord.

We will now examine two common voicings for D major and D minor. A D major chord contains the notes D-F♯-A.

```
D     E     F♯    G     A     B     C♯    D
⇑           ⇑           ⇑
1           3           5
```

To build a minor chord take the 1st, 3rd and 5th notes out of the major scale and lower the third by one semitone (formula 1-♭3-5). Therefore, a D minor chord would contain the notes D-F♮-A, the F♯ is lowered by one semitone.

D major
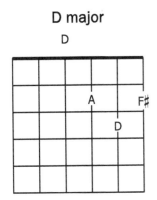

D minor
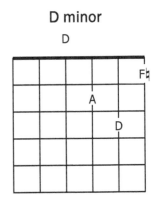

For E major and E minor you take out 1-3-5 from the E major scale:

```
E     F♯    G♯    A     B     C♯    D♯    E
⇑           ⇑           ⇑
1           3           5
```

The E minor chord requires E-G♮-B (1-♭3-5).

E major
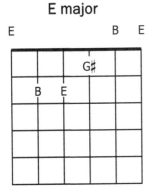

E minor
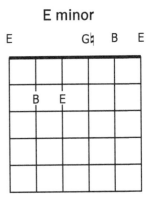

Absolute Essentials of Music Theory for Guitar

Basic Chords

Now we will examine some of the most common chord fingerings. The following chords are termed basic chords because they: (1) utilize open strings, (2) are among the first chords most guitar players should learn, and (3) are in fact the easiest chords to play for the beginning guitar player. To play these chords simply follow the fingerings shown below. The "X" symbol means to omit the string. The "O" indicates an open string that is part of the chord.

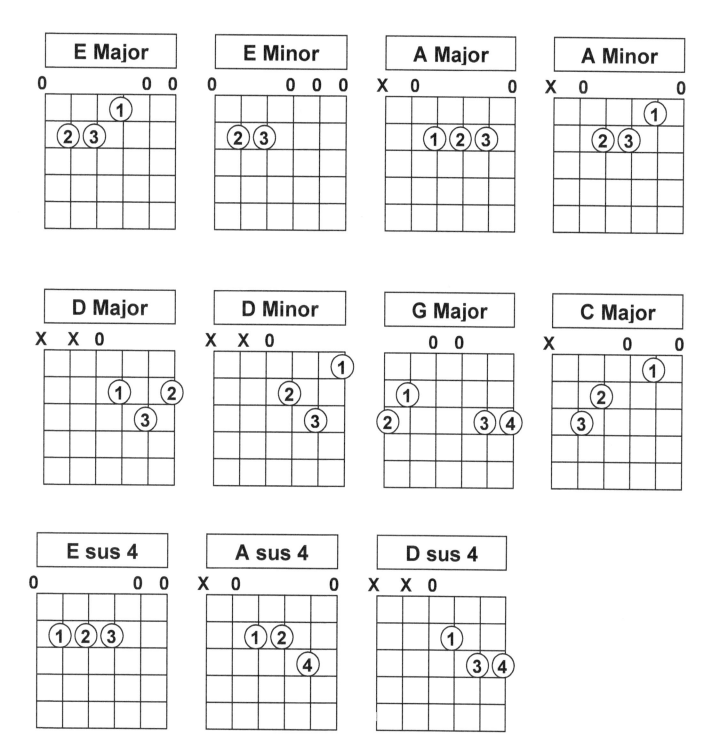

Moveable Chords

There is a world beyond the open string basic chords. These chords, referred to as moveable chords, are as their name implies—moveable. This means that you can take one chord shape and move it up or down the neck of the guitar to produce any desired chord. In other words, once you learn one of the moveable shapes for a major chord, you just have to move it up or down to produce 11 different major chords.

Here is how it works. We will take the major chord form that has a sixth string root note. **The black notes in each chord form represent the root notes.** The root note indicates the letter-name of the chord. If we move the 6th root major chord form so that the first finger is on the 8th fret, you will have a C major chord.

> When you see a chord that has the same finger on more than one string, it means that you must place this finger flat across all of the indicated strings. This is called a **barre** chord. To play the major barre chord shown below, you would place your first finger flat across all six strings. Next, place your second finger on the third string. Now position your third and fourth fingers on the fifth and fourth strings respectively. **In the barre chords shown in this book you are to play only the strings that have finger indications.** Since there are notes on every string of the chord shown below, you can strum all strings.

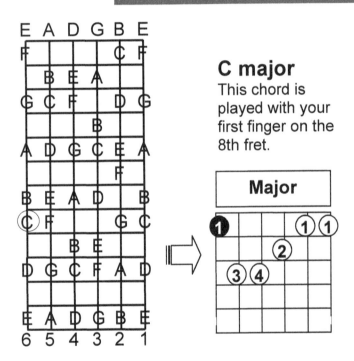

C major
This chord is played with your first finger on the 8th fret.

Major

Tip 1: If you find it hard to produce clear notes, practice barring with just your first finger. Place you first finger flat across all six strings and then pick each string. At first, you will have to exert a lot of pressure on the strings to get clear notes. Once your hands get stronger, and you get some good calluses on your fingers, you will find barre chords virtually effortless.

Tip 2: Experiment with finger placement. Shifting your barre finger up or down (i.e. perpendicular to the string) a millimetre or so, may make the difference between clear and muffled tones.

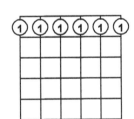

Now move this same chord shape so that the root note is on the first fret. Since the root note is on the note F, we now have an F major chord.

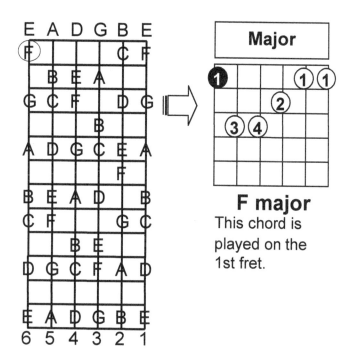

F major
This chord is played on the 1st fret.

As an additional example, consider what happens if we move this major chord up to the 4th fret: we will now have an Ab major chord. This chord could also be called a G♯ major chord. This is due to the fact that Ab and G♯ are both played on the same fret. These notes are referred to as *enharmonic equivalents*—they sound the same but are called two different things. Context is usually the factor that determines the correct letter-name of each chord.

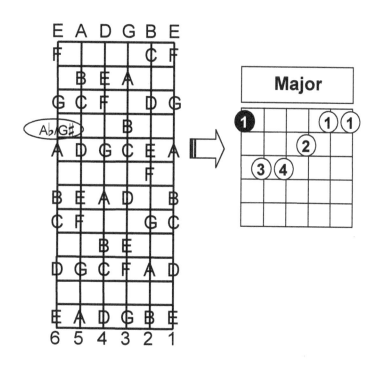

We will now look at a second way to play a major chord. In this example we will play C major with a fifth string root.

For this chord strum strings 5-4-3-2-1.

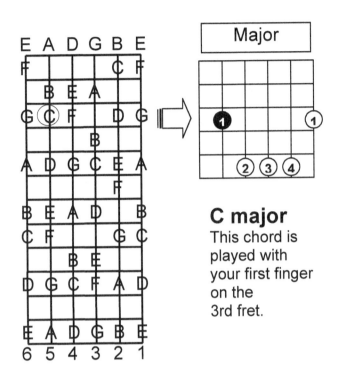

C major
This chord is played with your first finger on the 3rd fret.

In this example we will look at two ways to play B minor.

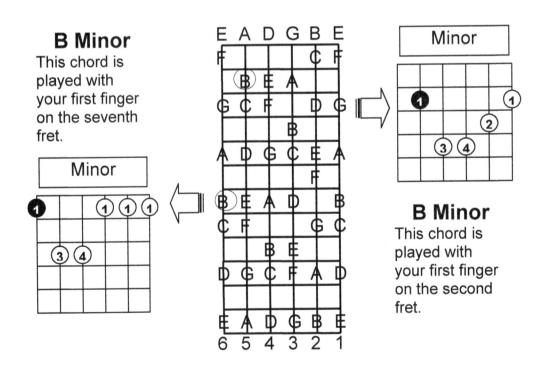

B Minor
This chord is played with your first finger on the seventh fret.

B Minor
This chord is played with your first finger on the second fret.

Absolute Essentials of Music Theory for Guitar

Below you will find moveable fingerings for the most common triads. Remember to play only the strings that have finger indications.

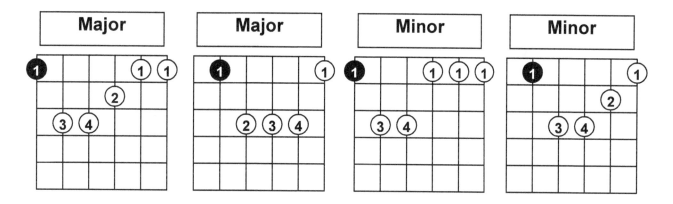

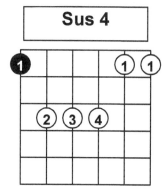

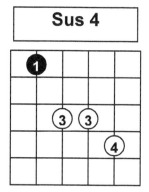

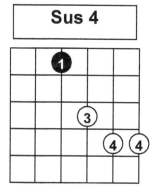

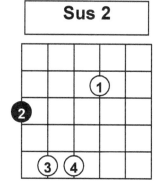

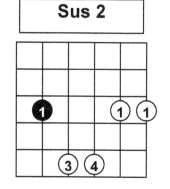

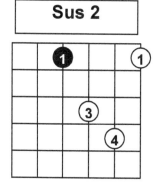

On the guitar any chord voicing that does not have open strings, can be considered a moveable chord. Chords that have open strings may be moveable as well, but they often require one too many fingers and frequently form difficult stretches. Below you will find basic voicings for each triad. As you can see there are no open strings so the chords can be moved to any fret. The root note in each chord is found on the fourth string and is shown in black. Practice playing these chords on each fret (i.e., chromatically). Play the minor triad on the first fret. This would be an F min chord. If you play the same chord shape on the second fret you will have an F♯ min chord.

Say and Play

As you play a moveable chord on different frets, make sure you say the pitch and chord quality out loud as the chord is sounded. Not only will this act as a great review for the notes on the fretboard, but this will also help you to memorize the root notes in each chord.

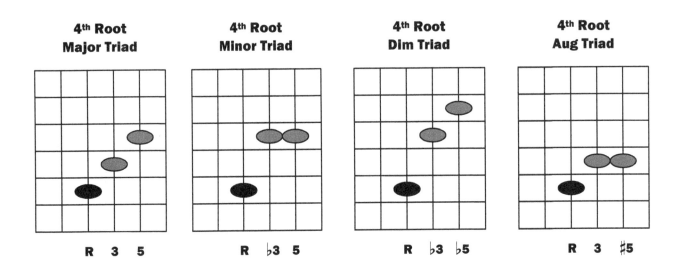

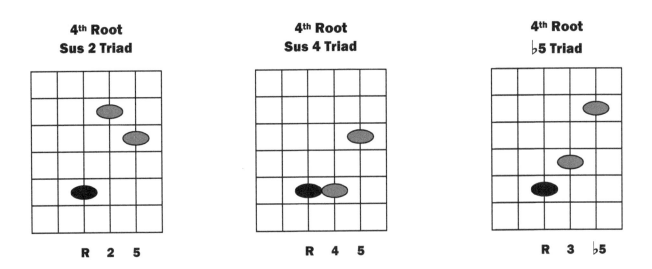

Absolute Essentials of Music Theory for Guitar

Major Triads

Below you will find moveable fingerings for root position, first inversion, and second inversion major triads. The root notes are shown in black. Simply move the appropriate fingering so that the root note is on the desired note.

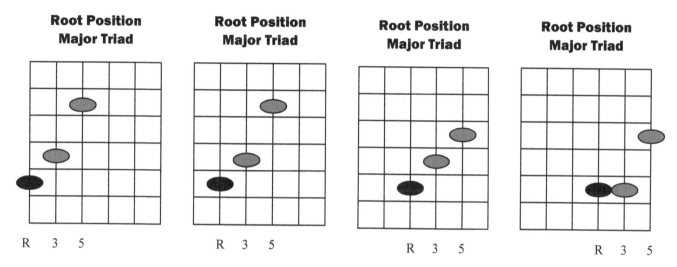

Root Position
Major Triad
R 3 5

Root Position
Major Triad
R 3 5

Root Position
Major Triad
R 3 5

Root Position
Major Triad
R 3 5

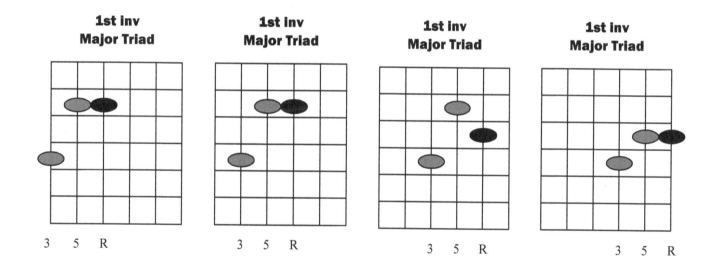

1st inv
Major Triad
3 5 R

1st inv
Major Triad
3 5 R

1st inv
Major Triad
3 5 R

1st inv
Major Triad
3 5 R

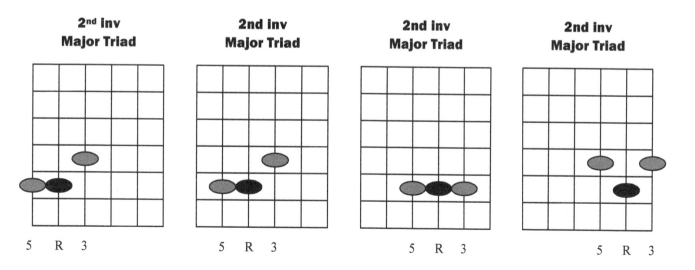

2nd inv
Major Triad
5 R 3

2nd inv
Major Triad
5 R 3

2nd inv
Major Triad
5 R 3

2nd inv
Major Triad
5 R 3

Minor Triads

Below you will find moveable fingerings for root position, first inversion, and second inversion minor triads. The root notes are shown in black. Simply move the appropriate fingering so that the root note is on the desired note.

Root Position
Minor Triad

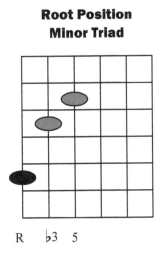

R ♭3 5

Root Position
Minor Triad

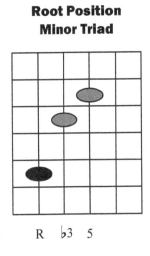

R ♭3 5

Root Position
Minor Triad

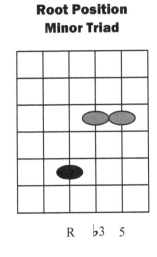

R ♭3 5

Root Position
Minor Triad

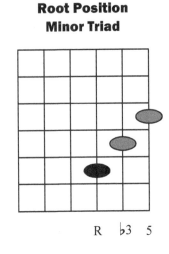

R ♭3 5

1st inv
Minor Triad

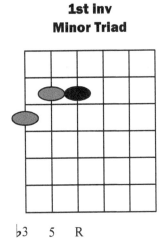

♭3 5 R

1st inv
Minor Triad

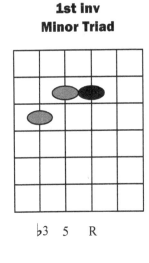

♭3 5 R

1st inv
Minor Triad

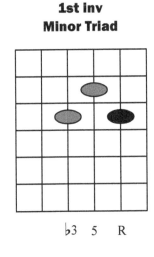

♭3 5 R

1st inv
Minor Triad

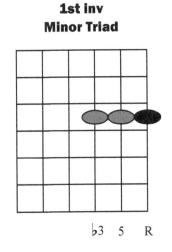

♭3 5 R

2nd inv
Minor Triad

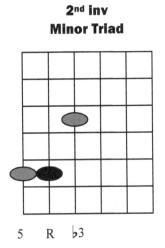

5 R ♭3

2nd inv
Minor Triad

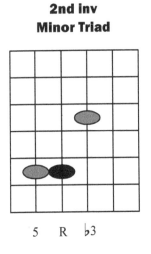

5 R ♭3

2nd inv
Minor Triad

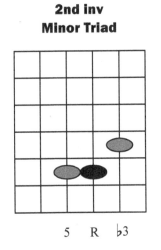

5 R ♭3

2nd inv
Minor Triad

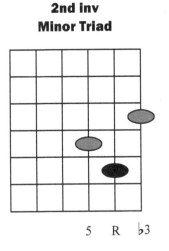

5 R ♭3

Absolute Essentials of Music Theory for Guitar

Diminished Triads

Below you will find moveable fingerings for root position, first inversion, and second inversion diminished triads. The root notes are shown in black. Simply move the appropriate fingering so that the root note is on the desired note.

Root Position Dim Triad   **Root Position Dim Triad**   **Root Position Dim Triad**   **Root Position Dim Triad**

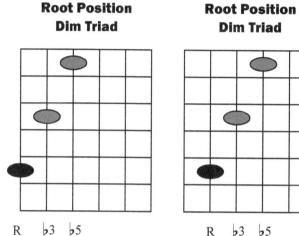 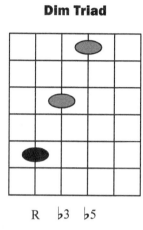 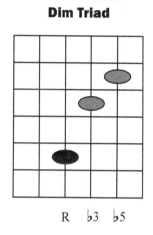 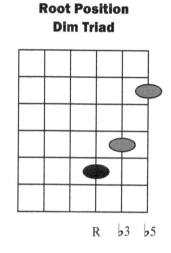

R   ♭3   ♭5   R   ♭3   ♭5   R   ♭3   ♭5   R   ♭3   ♭5

1st inv Dim Triad   **1st inv Dim Triad**   **1st inv Dim Triad**   **1st inv Dim Triad**

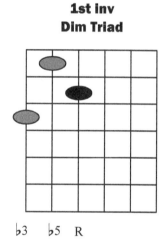 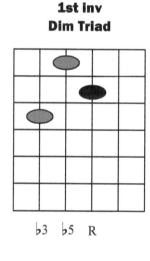 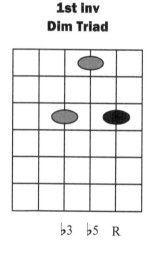 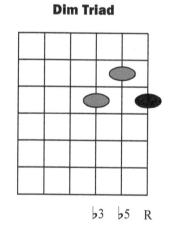

♭3   ♭5   R   ♭3   ♭5   R   ♭3   ♭5   R   ♭3   ♭5   R

2nd inv Dim Triad   **2nd inv Dim Triad**   **2nd inv Dim Triad**   **2nd inv Dim Triad**

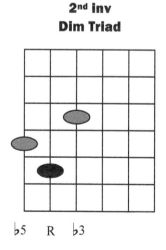 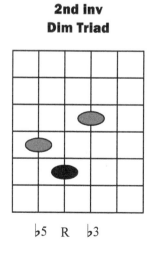 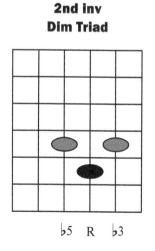 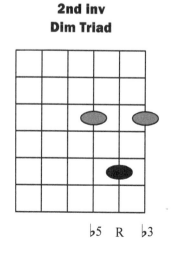

♭5   R   ♭3   ♭5   R   ♭3   ♭5   R   ♭3   ♭5   R   ♭3

Augmented Triads

Below you will find moveable fingerings for root position, first inversion, and second inversion augmented triads. The root notes are shown in black. Simply move the appropriate fingering so that the root note is on the desired note.

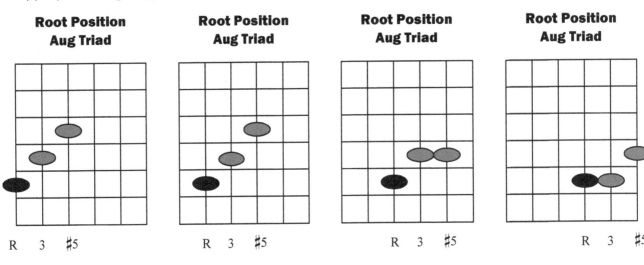

Root Position Aug Triad   R   3   ♯5

Root Position Aug Triad   R   3   ♯5

Root Position Aug Triad   R   3   ♯5

Root Position Aug Triad   R   3   ♯5

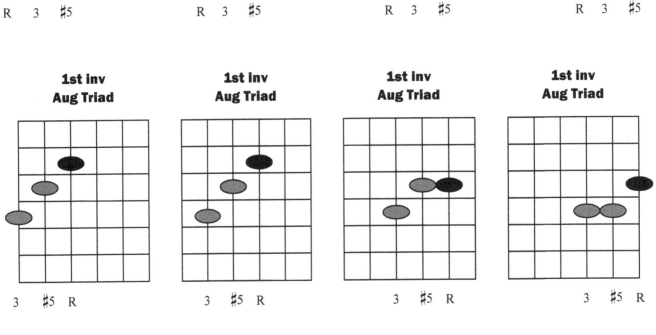

1st inv Aug Triad   3   ♯5   R

1st inv Aug Triad   3   ♯5   R

1st inv Aug Triad   3   ♯5   R

1st inv Aug Triad   3   ♯5   R

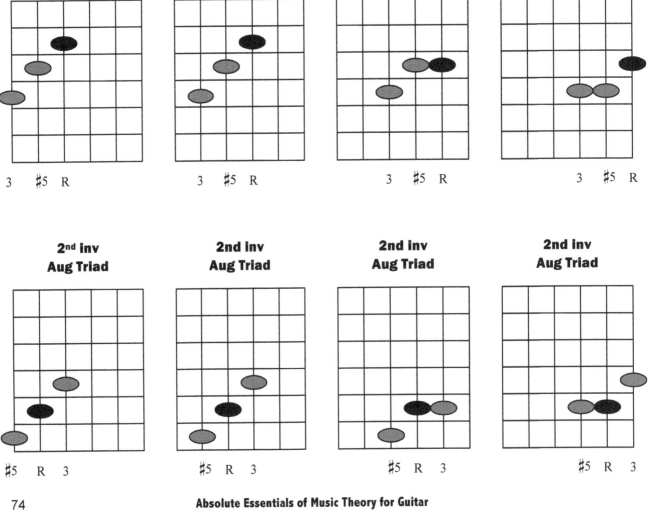

2nd inv Aug Triad   ♯5   R   3

2nd inv Aug Triad   ♯5   R   3

2nd inv Aug Triad   ♯5   R   3

2nd inv Aug Triad   ♯5   R   3

    Absolute Essentials of Music Theory for Guitar

Exercises

1. Identify the following chords:

2. In the treble clef notate the following chords:

    a) D min
    b) A dim
    c) B♭
    d) C aug
    e) G sus 2
    f) F♯
    g) A♭ dim
    h) B sus 4

3. Re-write the following chords in close position on the staff below and then identify the chord quality and position of both chords.

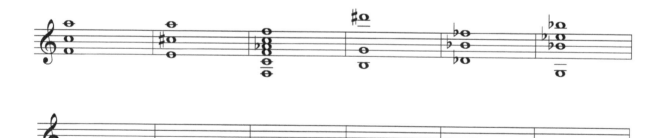

4. Practice moveable chords on the first twelve frets. As you play each chord say the letter name and chord quality out loud. For example, F major, F♯ major, G major, G♯ major, etc.

Answers

1.

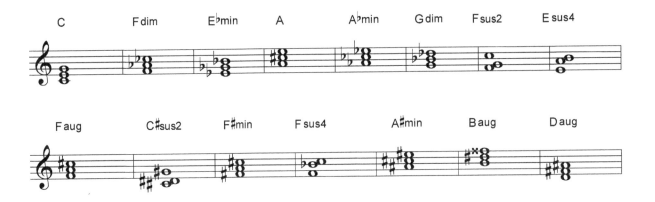

2.

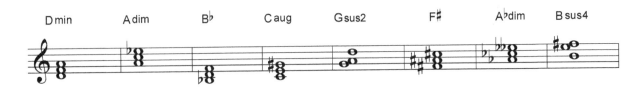

3.

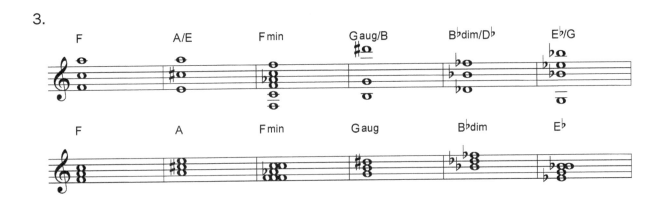

Absolute Essentials of Music Theory for Guitar

Chapter 5

Harmonized Scales

Chords can be built on each note of a scale. For example, if you were to write out a C major scale and build chords off of each degree, your result would be a harmonized major scale:

Diatonic Triads

To build chords on each degree of a scale you first write out the scale:

Now simply stack thirds on top of each scale degree:

Solving Triads

Here is how to determine the type of chord that is found on each note the major scale.

Step 1   Take the bottom note of the chord and compare the other notes of the chord to the major scale of the bottom note.

Step 2   Now compare the intervals to the triad formulas presented in chapter 4.

Take the bottom note of the chord and compare the chord tones to the major scale of this note. The bottom note in this example is a C, so you would compare the notes C-E-G to see if these notes are contained in the C major scale. Since they are contained in the C major scale, we know that they have not been altered in any way. The notes C-E-G are 1-3-5 in the key of C. The formula for a major triad is 1-3-5. Therefore this would be a C major triad.

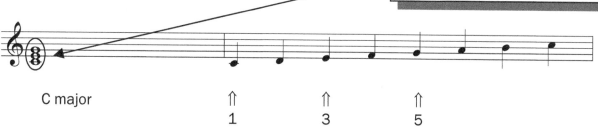

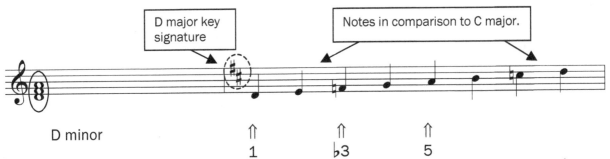

D minor ⇑ ⇑ ⇑
        1 ♭3 5

For this chord the notes are D-F-A. If we look at the notes in the D major scale (D-E-F♯-G-A-B-C♯), we see that the F and C are both sharp. The notes in the chord are D-F-A. Therefore, the F has been lowered by one semitone. We end up with 1-♭3-5, forming a D minor chord. Remember that the chords we are examining here are built off of each note of the C major scale. The C major scale has no sharps or flats.

E minor ⇑ ⇑ ⇑
        1 ♭3 5

Now compare the notes E-G-B to the E major scale (E-F♯-G♯-A-B-C♯-D♯). Here we see that the G should be sharp to form an E major triad. The third has been lowered by a semitone so the result is, E min: E-G-B, 1-♭3-5.

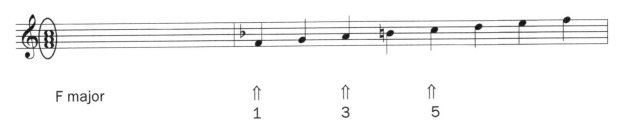

F major ⇑ ⇑ ⇑
        1 3 5

The notes in this chord are F-A-C. These notes can be found in the F major scale. The B is the only note that is flat in F major (F-G-A-B♭-C-D-E). Since there is no B in this chord, the notes have not been altered. Our result is 1-3-5, F-A-C. Therefore this is an F major chord.

G major ⇑ ⇑ ⇑
        1 3 5

We now go to G major. The G major scale has one sharp, an F♯ (G-A-B-C-D-E-F♯). The notes in this chord are G-B-D. The F is not contained in this chord, so none of the notes have been altered, meaning we have a G major triad, 1-3-5.

A minor   ⇑   ⇑   ⇑
                       1   ♭3   5

The six chord (VI) in C major is an A min. This is derived from the fact that A major contains the notes A-B-C#-D-E-F#-G#-A. The chord tones are A-C-E. This means that the third has been lowered by one semitone. The result is 1-♭3-5, A-C-E, an A minor chord.

B dim   ⇑   ⇑   ⇑
                       1   ♭3   ♭5

The notes in B major are: B-C#-D#-E-F#-G#-A#-B. The VII chord in C major consists of the notes B-D-F. If this was a B maj triad it would contain B-D#-F#. Since we have B-D-F, it means that each note has been lowered by one semitone. If you consult the formulas in chapter 4 you will see that the 1-♭3-♭5 constitutes a diminished triad.

In the previous chapter we used black notes to indicate the root notes in chord diagrams. This was done purely as a visual aid. In sheet music you will see all chord tones indicated as black notes and open strings indicated with an "O".

Below you will see the chords contained in C, G, D and A major scales. Can you see any patterns?

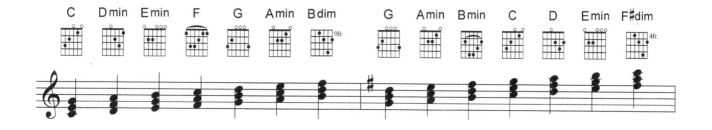

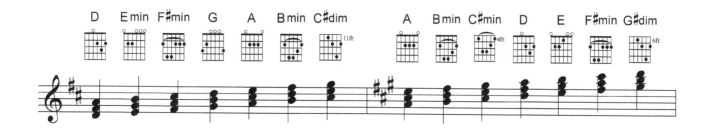

Notice that the chords built on the first, fourth and fifth degrees are all major chords. The chords built on the second, third and sixth degrees are minor. A chord built on the seventh note of the scale is diminished. This is a consistent pattern encountered in all major scales.

I	**Major**
II	**Minor**
III	**Minor**
IV	**Major**
V	**Major**
VI	**Minor**
VII	**Diminished**

Roman Numerals
A chord's position in a key is usually symbolized with a Roman numeral. Some theorists prefer to use upper-case Roman numerals for the one (I), four (IV), and five (V) chords. Lower-case numerals are used for the remaining chords in the key. Classical theorists will often use upper-case Roman numerals for major and augmented chords and lower-case for minor and diminished chords. Most contemporary theorists use all upper-case Roman numerals for chords, regardless of their position in the key. We will use all upper-case Roman numerals.

Using the above pattern of chords, you can quickly determine the chords in any major scale. Let's say you need to know the chords found in E major. The notes in E major are E-F♯-G♯-A-B-C♯-D♯-E. Using the above formula our result is:

I	E major
II	F♯ minor
III	G♯ minor
IV	A major
V	B major
VI	C♯ minor
VII	D♯ diminished

Roman Numerals Review
Just in case you are a bit rusty on Roman numerals, here is a quick review.

Roman Numeral	Arabic Numeral
I, i	1
II, ii	2
III, iii	3
IV, iv	4
V, v	5
VI, vi	6
VII, vii	7
VIII, viii	8

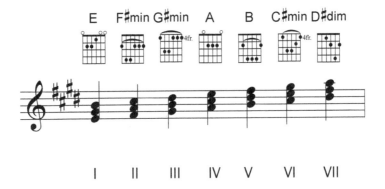

On the following pages you will find all of the triads in every major scale.

Harmonized Major Scales

Harmonized Major Scales

Absolute Essentials of Music Theory for Guitar

Application

Below you will find the triads of C major and G major scales tabbed out.

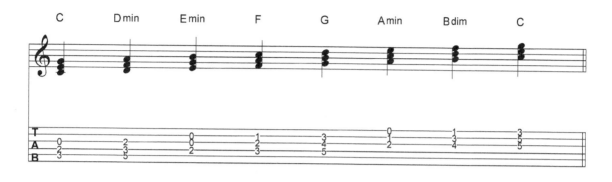

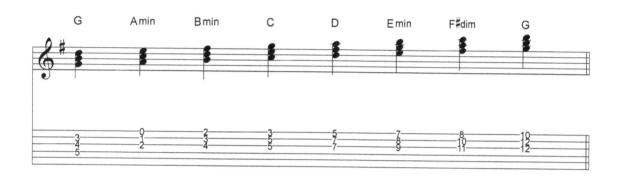

Generally it is much more practical to use common chord voicings for the harmonized scales. The harmonized scales tell you what chords belong in a given key. You can use any chord voicings you desire. On pages 84 and 85 you will see some of the many possible ways to play the triads in each major scale. Be sure to experiment with different voicings.

Absolute Essentials of Music Theory for Guitar

Absolute Essentials of Music Theory for Guitar

Chord Progression

A **chord progression** is the term used to describe the movement of two or more chords. Chord progressions are usually denoted with Roman numerals based on the numeric position of the chord within the key. The primary reason for using Roman numerals is that it makes it easy to transpose a progression to multiple keys. Consider a I—V—I chord progression. In the key of C major the progression would be C—G—C. In G major a I—V—I is G—D—G, while in A major, the progression would be A—E—A.

Here are some common chord progressions. Experiment with different voicings and also create your own progressions.

I—IV—V

I—VI—II—V

III—VI—II—V

II—V—I

As you play these chord progressions you will recognize countless songs. Be sure to practice the progressions in every key.

Absolute Essentials of Music Theory for Guitar

You can also build triads on each degree of the minor, harmonic minor and melodic minor scales.

Natural Minor Triads

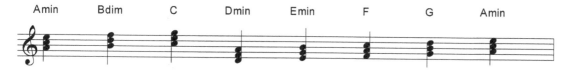

The triads in minor also follow a pattern. The following is true in all minor keys:

I	Min
II	Dim
III	Maj
IV	Min
V	Min
VI	Maj
VII	Maj

Harmonic Minor Triads

In harmonic minor the following is true:

I	Min
II	Dim
III	Aug
IV	Min
V	Maj
VI	Maj
VII	Dim

Jazz Minor Triads

In jazz minor the following is true:

I	Min
II	Min
III	Aug
IV	Maj
V	Maj
VI	Dim
VII	Dim

On the following six pages you will find the triads for all natural minor, harmonic minor and jazz minor keys. The chords are presented with symbols and chord diagrams. You will find open string and barre chord voicings for the chords. Remember that these voicings are just some of the many possibilities. Feel free to experiment with different voicings.

Harmonized Natural Minor Scales

Harmonized Natural Minor Scales

Absolute Essentials of Music Theory for Guitar

Harmonized Harmonic Minor Scales

Harmonized Harmonic Minor Scales

Harmonized Jazz Minor Scales

Harmonized Jazz Minor Scales

Absolute Essentials of Music Theory for Guitar

Exercises

1. Identify the following chords:

    a) What is the II chord in A major _____
    b) What is the I chord in A♭ major _____
    c) What is the V chord in B major _____
    d) What is the III chord in F major _____
    e) What is the II chord in D♭ major _____
    f) What is the VI chord in C♯ major _____
    g) What is the II chord in G major _____
    h) What is the VII chord in A major _____
    i) What is the IV chord in E major _____
    j) What is the V chord in D major _____
    k) What is the III chord in F♯ major _____
    l) What is the III chord in F♯ minor _____
    m) What is the I chord in F♯ harm min _____
    n) What is the VII chord in D minor _____
    o) What is the V chord in G jazz min _____
    p) What is the IV chord in E harm min _____

2. In the treble clef write all of the triads in:

    a) G major
    b) F major
    c) B♭ major
    d) D min
    e) B major
    f) C harmonic minor
    g) F jazz minor

Answers

1. Identify the following chords:
    a) What is the II chord in A major   _____B min
    b) What is the I chord in A♭ major   _____A♭
    c) What is the V chord in B major   _____F♯
    d) What is the III chord in F major   _____A min
    e) What is the II chord in D♭ major   _____E♭ min
    f) What is the VI chord in C♯ major   _____A♯ min
    g) What is the II chord in G major   _____A min
    h) What is the VII chord in A major   _____G♯ dim
    i) What is the IV chord in E major   _____A
    j) What is the V chord in D major   _____A
    k) What is the III chord in F♯ major   _____A♯ min
    l) What is the III chord in F♯ minor   _____A
    m) What is the I chord in F♯ harm min _____F♯ min
    n) What is the VII chord in D minor   _____C
    o) What is the V chord in G jazz min   _____D
    p) What is the IV chord in E harm min _____A min

2. In the treble clef write all of the triads in:
    a) G major

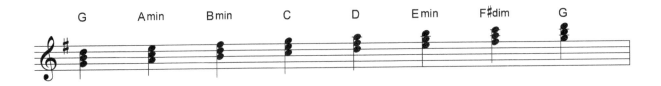

    b) F major

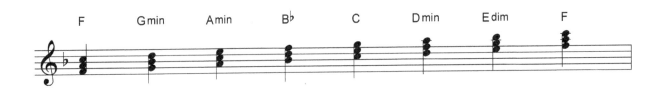

    c) B♭ major

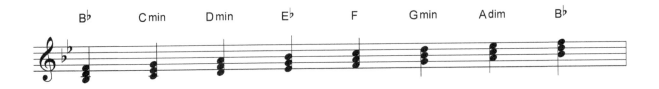

d) D min

e) B major

f) C harmonic minor

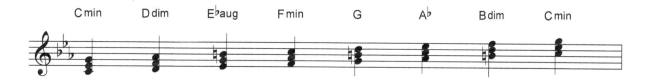

g) F jazz minor

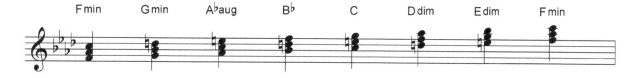

Chapter 6

Rhythm

Levels of Rhythmic Activity

Music is usually organized in a repeatable accent pattern known as meter. In free time, music unfolds with an unpredictable accent pattern (i.e. there are no regular recurring accents). If a performer plays a note, then several others quickly, then pauses for a while and plays additional notes, you would have an example of free time. This means that there is no time signature being used. If we were to notate this example with vertical slashes, here is what we would have:

```
    >             >
    |          ||| | |              | ||
```

The vertical slashes represent the notes and the distance between each slash represents time. The accent symbol (>) indicates the notes that are emphasized or accented.

Pulse/Beat

You will occasionally encounter music where each beat is an equal distance apart, but the accent pattern does not appear to repeat. In this instance you have music that has an unpredictable occurrence of strong and weak beats. Strong beats are very definite, while weak beats are of a more subtle nature.

S   W   S   S   S   W   W   S   W etc.

S = strong
W = weak

Meter

When you have a recurring repeatable accent pattern, you have meter. The repeatable accent pattern will consist of a combination of strong and weak beats. For example:

2/4 time consists of:
S   W

3/4 time consists of:
S   W   W

4/4 time consists of:
S   W   M   W (M stands for medium weak)

5/4 time consists of:
S   W   S   W   W
or
S   W   W   S   W

Time Values

The most common time signature, 4/4, (pronounced four-four) is often abbreviated with a fancy "C" and called common time. In 4/4, the whole note receives four beats or counts. The half note receives two beats and the quarter note receives one beat. Eighth notes each receive half of a beat.

or

Note Durations

Note Durations

Eighth notes are sometimes written without connecting beams:

The whole note receives 4 beats; the half note receives 2 beats; a quarter note receives 1 beat and an eighth note receives half of a beat; a sixteenth note receives one quarter of a beat and the triplet receives one third of a beat.

Sixteenth notes   **Triplets**

1 e & ah 2 e & ah 3 e & ah 4 e & ah   1 & ah 2 & ah 3 & ah 4 & ah

Rest Durations

Silence is notated with rests:

Rest Durations

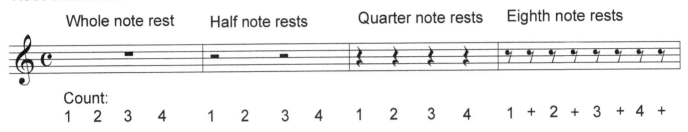

Whole note rest	Half note rests	Quarter note rests	Eighth note rests

Count:
1 2 3 4   1 2 3 4   1 2 3 4   1 + 2 + 3 + 4 +

Sixteenth note rests

1 e + ah 2 e + ah 3 e + ah 4 e + ah

Dotted and Tied Notes

Tie
⇓

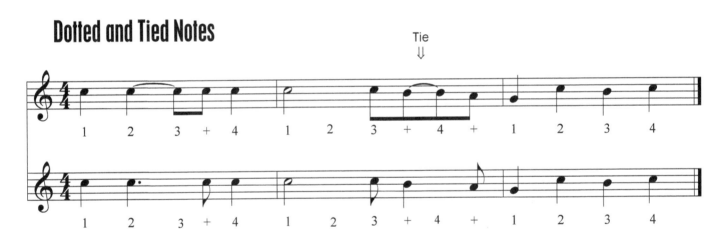

Ties and dots are used to increase the time value of the notes they follow. A **dot** increases the time value of a note by half. A half note receives 2 beats; a dotted half note receives 3 beats. A quarter note receives one beat; a dotted quarter note receives one and a half beats. An eighth note receives half of a beat; a dotted eighth note receives half of a beat plus one quarter of a beat (in other words 3/4's of a beat).

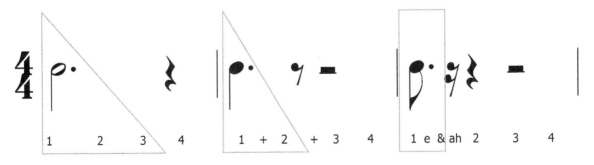

Absolute Essentials of Music Theory for Guitar

The notes in a tie are of the same pitch. A **tie** increases the time value of a note by the value of the second note. You do not sound the second note of the tie. You simply sustain the note for the duration of the first note plus the value of note it is tied to.

Repeats

Instead of writing out the same music twice, repeats are used.

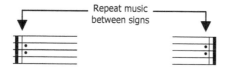

First and Second Endings

To perform first and second endings, the passage is repeated but the ending is different the second time.

Time Signatures

A time signature is used to indicate the strong and weak beats in a measure and also which note value receives one beat. The note that receives one beat is referred to as the **pulse note**. In **simple time** (2/2, 2/4, 2/8, 3/2, 3/4, 3/8, 4/2, 4/4, 4/8), the top number of the time signature indicates the number of beats per measure while the bottom number indicates the type of note that receives one beat (pulse note). For example:

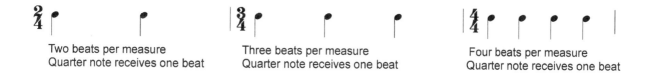

Two beats per measure
Quarter note receives one beat

Three beats per measure
Quarter note receives one beat

Four beats per measure
Quarter note receives one beat

In simple time you tap your foot on each beat. In **compound time**, (6/4, 6/8, 6/16, 9/4, 9/8, 9/16, 12/4, 12/8, 12/16) it is best to tap your foot on each major beat division. In 6/8 time the measure is divided into two (1 2 3), (4 5 6). Nine-eight time has three main divisions (1 2 3), (4 5 6), (7 8 9). Twelve-eight time is comprised of 4 main divisions (1 2 3), (4 5 6), (7 8 9), (10 11 12). In 6/8 you would count **1** 2 3 **4** 5 6, but only tap your foot on 1 and 4. In 9/8 you would count **1** 2 3 **4** 5 6 **7** 8 9, and tap your foot on 1, 4, and 7. In 12/8 time you count **1** 2 3 **4** 5 6 **7** 8 9 **10** 11 12, and tap your foot on 1, 4, 7, and 10.

When you look at the time signature 6/8, it may appear that there are six beats per measure and the eighth note receives one beat. In compound meters, pulse notes are dotted notes and can therefore be divided into three parts. Any type of dotted note can be the pulse note in a compound meter, but the most common is the dotted quarter note.

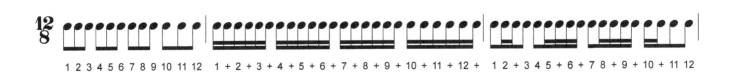

Application

Rhythm guitar parts are often notated with slashes or rhythmic notation. This makes reading chord parts easy. All you do is play the appropriate chord with the notated rhythm. The slashes represent the chords while the stems indicate the time values of the chords. Depending on the notation, you may or may not, see down-strokes and/or up-strokes notated.

⊓ ⇒ down-stroke   V ⇒ up-stroke

Generally, down-strokes are used on the beat, so they would be used on the 1, 2, 3, 4, in four-four time. The upstroke is usually used on the up-beat or the "ands" of each beat.

The slashes shown below are quarter notes so you would count each one as a beat.

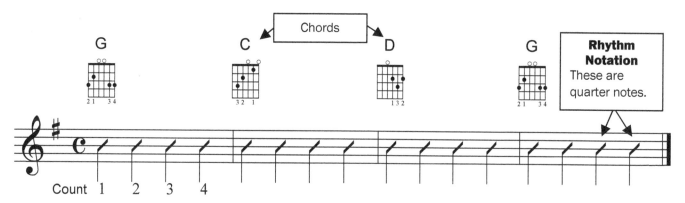

As you can see by the time signature, the chord progression is in common time or 4/4. For this chord study use only down-strokes. Simply strum each chord with a down-stroke on the beat.

The next chord progression makes use of up and down-strokes.

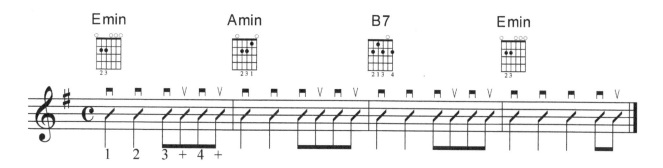

Now that you are familiar with the basics of time, take some of the chord voicings covered in chapters 4 and 5 and experiment with different rhythms and strumming patterns.

Exercises

1.   Add time signatures for the following examples:

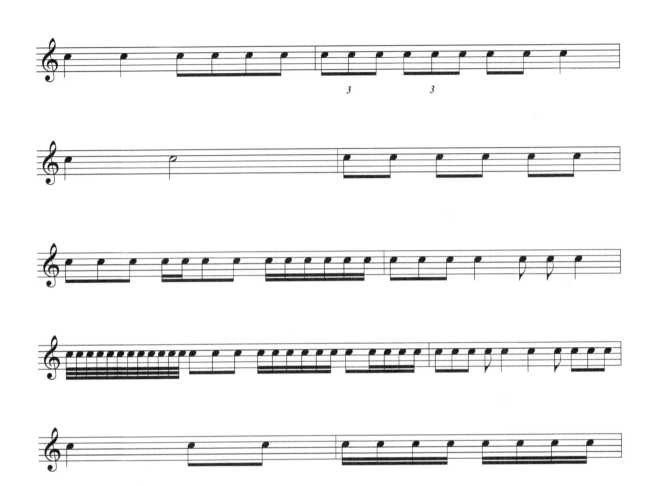

Absolute Essentials of Music Theory for Guitar

Answers

1.

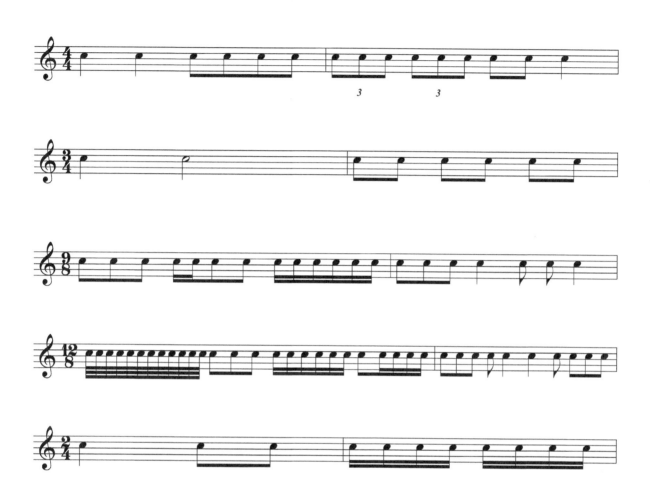

Conclusion

Congratulations! You now know the absolute essentials of music theory. This book has examined a lot of information. Remember that the key to long term retention of this information is application. Apply the contents of this book to the guitar and to the analysis of the music you listen to and play. In addition, you should create your own questions for the concepts that have been covered in this book. For example:

- Using letter-names, write all of the major scales that contain one or more flat.
- Using letter-names, write all of the major scales that contain one or more sharp.
- Play the A major scale on the fourth string.
- What major scale contains two sharps?
- What major scale contains five sharps?
- What natural minor scale contains no flats?
- What natural minor scale contains six sharps?
- What natural minor scale contains four flats?
- Play G natural minor ascending and descending on the fifth string.
- Using letter-names, write a B harmonic minor scale.
- Using letter-names, write an F♯ harmonic minor scale.
- Using letter-names, write a D melodic minor scale.
- Using letter-names, write a D jazz minor scale.
- What is the relative minor of G major?
- What is the relative major of G minor?
- What is the relative minor of D major?
- What is the relative minor of E♭ major?
- What are the notes in a D minor chord?
- What notes make up a G major chord?
- Play a voicing for an A♭ major in first inversion.

You can also work on your understanding of music when you are away from your instrument. Work on mental drills when you don't have the guitar handy. For example, ask yourself: "What major scale contains five flats?" "What are the notes in a B♭ major scale?" "What notes are found in a D diminished triad?" Practice reciting the notes in scales ascending and descending. Name all of the triads contained in each major scale, etc. Visualize yourself playing a D harmonic minor scale. As you "see" yourself playing these notes also hear what the notes would sound like. Using this "down time" to mentally practice theory will enable you to master theory and allow you to devote most of your practice time to actually playing the guitar.

Index

Absolute Essentials of Music Theory for Guitar

Also by Don J. MacLean

Absolute Essentials of Music Theory for all Instruments

Just what you absolutely need to know! In this easy-to-follow self-study guide, are all the need to know basics, demystified, chapter-by-chapter. Discover how easy it is to understand: music notation, scales, intervals, chords, harmonized scales, and rhythm. For all instruments, beginner to intermediate. Answer key included.
$19.99, ISBN 1-896595-12-X, 69 pages, 8½ X 11

Absolute Essentials of Music Theory for Guitar

This book will show you how to totally understand guitar theory super-fast! Change how you see music theory with the Absolute Essentials of Music Theory for Guitar. This easy-to-follow guide shows you the need to know basics, demystified, chapter-by-chapter. Discover how easy it is to understand: reading music, the fretboard, scales, intervals, chords, harmonized scales and rhythm. Music theory has never been easier! All theoretical concepts are applied to the guitar. Test yourself answer key included. What are you waiting for? Your understanding of music theory starts here!
$22.99, ISBN 1-896595-32-4, 112 pages, 8½ X 11

Guitar Essentials: Scale Master Expanded Edition

The key to 1004 scales! With Guitar Essentials: Scale Master Expanded Edition you will discover how easy it is to master scales. Learn 16 scale types with 92 fingerings transposed to all keys for a total of 1004 scales. This expanded edition provides you with tips and short-cuts that make learning scales a snap. Scales have never made more sense.
$19.99, ISBN 1-896595-26-X, 75 pages, 8½ X 11

Guitar Essentials: Chord Master Expanded Edition

Make an instant impact on your playing with Guitar Essentials: Chord Master Expanded Edition. Loaded with new features, this expanded edition is easy-to-understand and perfect for all styles of music. Learn how to play 36 basic chords and 95 moveable chords in all 12 keys, for a total of 1176 chords.
$17.99, ISBN 1-896595-24-3, 51 pages, 8½ X 11

Guitar Essentials: Chord Master

Laminated Reference Chart
Guitar Essentials: Chord Master shows guitarists of all levels how to quickly and easily play 1176 of the most common guitar chords. This is the ultimate guitar chord cheat-sheet!
$4.99, ISBN 1-896595-13-8,1 Double sided page, 8½ X 11

Guitar Essentials: Scale Master 1
Laminated Reference Chart
Guitar Essentials: Scale Master 1 shows you how to play the most common scales. Major, minor, harmonic minor, melodic minor, major pentatonic, minor pentatonic, blues and the composite blues scales are all included in this chart.
$4.99, ISBN 1-896595-30-8,1 Double sided page; 8½ X 11

Guitar Essentials: Improviser
Laminated Reference Chart
Guitar Essentials: Improviser provides the intermediate guitarist with the tools to improvise over chords. Start with a scale and view the chords that can be used or, select a chord and view its scale options. All scale forms are shown in transposable neck diagrams. The Improviser is the first chart to provide guitar players with easy access to this information and is the perfect companion to The World of Scales.
$7.99 CDN/$6.99 USD, ISBN 1-896595-19-7, 1 Double sided page; 11 X 17

Music Essentials: Improviser
Laminated Reference Chart
Music Essentials: Improviser provides the intermediate musician with the tools to improvise over chords. Start with a scale and view the chords that can be used or, select a chord and view its scale options. All scales are shown in treble and bass clefs. The Improviser is the first chart to provide musicians with easy access to this information and is the perfect companion to The World of Scales.
$7.99 CDN/$6.99 USD, ISBN 1-896595-23-5,1 Double-sided page; 11 X 17

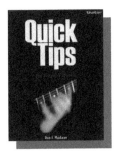

Quick Tips for Faster Fingers
Wouldn't you rather play faster, more accurately and with better technique? Add a new dimension to your guitar playing with 54 specially chosen and created technique builders for massive chops. Whether you are a beginner or intermediate guitar player, you will refer to this text again and again. Includes audio CD.
$24.99, ISBN 1-896595-10-3, 62 pages, 8½ X 11, Book and Audio CD

Quick Tips: Guitar Technique 101
Quick Tips: Guitar Technique 101, contains 36 specially created exercises and 7 pieces for massive chops. This book shows you foundation exercises that will increase your speed, strength and accuracy.
$9.99, ISBN 1-896595-25-1, 52 pages, 5½ X 8.5

Quick Tips: Guitar Chords 101

Don't let the compact size fool you! Quick Tips: Guitar Chords 101, will show you all the essential guitar chords you need to play your favourite songs. Discover how easy it is to play: basic chords, power chords, barre chords, and basic chord progressions.

$9.99, ISBN 1-896595-27-8, 60 pages, 5½ X 8.5

Guitar Quick Start

Here is everything you need to start playing today. No experience necessary. Guitar Quick Start will show you how easy it is to play guitar. This book will take you from basic chords and scales to their ultimate application: playing songs. You don't just read this book, you play it. Hear it then play it, companion audio CD included. Less work, more play!

$22.99, ISBN 1-896595-28-6, 108 pages, 8½ X 11, Book and Audio CD

World of Scales: A Compendium of Scales for the Modern Guitar Player

The World of Scales: A Compendium of Scales for the Modern Guitar Player shows guitarists of all levels how scales can be used. The World of Scales provides the reader with the most comprehensive examination of scales available. All scales are shown in easy-to-read and transposable fingerings.

$25.95 CDN/$19.95 USD, ISBN 1-896595-07-3, 165 pages, 8½ X 11

World of Scales: A Compendium of Scales for all Instruments

The World of Scales: A Compendium of Scales for all Instruments enables intermediate to advanced musicians to understand: how scales are built; how chords are constructed and interact with scales; how to apply modalization to any scale. The World of Scales provides the reader with the most thorough examination of scales available. All scales are shown in treble and bass clefs.

$25.95 CDN/$19.95 USD, ISBN 1-896595-21-9, 96 pages, 8½ X 11

Absolute Essentials of Guitar

Just what you absolutely need to know! When you just want to play the guitar, the Absolute Essentials are all you need. Discover how easy it is to: tune the guitar, practice for maximum results, master the fretboard, read music, play chords, play scales, play the blues and play songs. Is this all possible? Absolutely.

$25.99, ISBN 1-896595-14-6, 113 pages, 8½ X 11, Book and Audio CD

Mega Chops: Scale Mastery Beyond Hanon for Guitar

The Hanon Studies have long been a staple in technique development for the pianist. Now, these highly effective exercises can be applied to the guitar to give you an excellent workout that will improve your technique and mastery of the guitar.

Mega Chops: Scale Mastery Beyond Hanon, will show you virtually limitless ways to practice scales and improve your technique. You'll discover: 44 highly effective technique exercises for all finger groups; 27 Hanon Studies organized in increasing difficulty for the guitarist; fingerings for the most popular scales; the most common melodic patterns; proven ways to create and use melodic patterns; and how to play the Hanon Studies, or any melodic pattern, over the entire fretboard in every key.

$24.99, ISBN 1-896595-20-0, 120 pages, 8½ X 11

Check your leading book/music store or,
visit us online at:
www.agogic.biz

ORDER FORM
Order 2 or more products to receive *FREE* shipping!!!

AEMTG

Canadian Order Form

Free shipping when you order 2 or more titles

Prices shown in Canadian dollars	Price	Shipping	GST	TOTAL	Qty.
World of Scales for Guitar	$ 25.95	free	$ 1.82	$ 27.77	
World of Scales for all Inst	$ 25.95	free	$ 1.82	$ 27.77	
Guitar Essentials: Chord Master	$ 4.99	free	$ 0.35	$ 5.34	
Guitar Essentials: Scale Master 1	$ 4.99	free	$ 0.35	$ 5.34	
Guitar Essentials: Improviser	$ 7.99	free	$ 0.56	$ 8.55	
Music Essentials: Improviser	$ 7.99	free	$ 0.56	$ 8.55	
Guitar Essentials: Chord Master Exp. Ed.	$ 17.99	free	$ 1.26	$ 19.25	
Guitar Essentials: Scale Master Exp. Ed.	$ 19.99	free	$ 1.40	$ 21.39	
Absolute Essentials of Music Theory	$ 19.99	free	$ 1.40	$ 21.39	
Absolute Essentials of Music Theory for Guitar	$ 22.99	free	$ 1.61	$ 24.60	
Absolute Essentials of Guitar	$ 25.99	free	$ 1.82	$ 27.81	
Mega Chops: Scale Mastery Beyond Hanon	$ 24.99	free	$ 1.75	$ 26.74	
Quick Tips for Faster Fingers	$ 24.99	free	$ 1.75	$ 26.74	
Quick Tips: Guitar Technique 101	$ 9.99	free	$ 0.70	$ 10.69	
Quick Tips: Guitar Chords 101	$ 9.99	free	$ 0.70	$ 10.69	
Guitar Quick Start	$ 22.99	free	$ 1.61	$ 24.60	
				TOTAL Qty.	

To order an individual title, please add $5.00 for shipping plus G.S.T.

Ship To:

Name

Address

City/ Prov

Postal Code

Phone

Email

Mail this order form today with your certified cheque or money order payable to:

Agogic Publishing
406-109 Tenth Street
New Westminster, BC
V3M 3X7
Phone 604-290-2692
Fax 604-540-4419
Prices subject to change without notice. Online pricing may vary.

Check your leading book/music store or,
visit us online at:
www.agogic.biz

ORDER FORM

Order 2 or more products to receive *FREE* shipping!!!

AEMTG

U.S. Order Form

Free shipping when you order 2 or more titles

Prices shown in U.S. dollars	Price	Shipping	TOTAL	Qty.
World of Scales for Guitar	$ 19.95	free	$19.95	
World of Scales for all Inst	$ 19.95	free	$19.95	
Guitar Essentials: Chord Master	$ 4.99	free	$ 4.99	
Guitar Essentials: Scale Master 1	$ 4.99	free	$ 4.99	
Guitar Essentials: Improviser	$ 6.99	free	$ 6.99	
Music Essentials: Improviser	$ 6.99	free	$ 6.99	
Guitar Essentials: Chord Master Exp. Ed.	$ 17.99	free	$17.99	
Guitar Essentials: Scale Master Exp. Ed.	$ 19.99	free	$19.99	
Absolute Essentials of Music Theory	$ 19.99	free	$19.99	
Absolute Essentials of Music Theory for Guitar	$ 22.99	free	$22.99	
Absolute Essentials of Guitar	$ 25.99	free	$ 25.99	
Mega Chops: Scale Mastery Beyond Hanon	$ 24.99	free	$24.99	
Quick Tips for Faster Fingers	$ 24.99	free	$24.99	
Quick Tips: Guitar Technique 101	$ 9.99	free	$ 9.99	
Quick Tips: Guitar Chords 101	$ 9.99	free	$ 9.99	
Guitar Quick Start	$ 22.99	free	$ 22.99	
To order an individual title, please add $6.00 for shipping.			TOTAL Qty.	

Ship To:

Name _____

Address _____

City/State _____

Zip Code _____

Phone _____

Email _____

Mail this order form today with your certified cheque or money order payable to:

Agogic Publishing
406-109 Tenth Street
New Westminster, BC
V3M 3X7
Phone 604-290-2692
Fax 604-540-4419
Prices subject to change without notice. Online pricing may vary.